The Mysteries of Ephesos

I0078920

Adrian Anderson PhD

What acolytes experienced at Ephesos.
Rudolf Steiner's research into the
Artemis-Diana Mysteries.

Threshold Publishing, Australia, 2021
www.rudolfsteinerstudies.com

Distributed by Ebooks Alchemy
Prahran East VIC 3198
Australia

ISBN 978-0-6451954-0-8

.

The Ephesian Mystery

The human being is a Microcosm formed from the Macrocosm; so the human being carries within itself the secrets of the Cosmos.

The Word, the Logos, spoke forth Creation.

"So study the Human Secret in the little words, in the Micro-logos, thereby you shall become ready to feel within you the Secret of the Macro-logos": (Ephesian hierophant)

Rudolf Steiner, Dec 2nd. 1923

Illustration 1: A statue of Artemis-Diana as the matrix of the creative fertility of the Earth.

Foreword

What was it that justified the building of a temple so magnificent and so revered that it was spared destruction from wars and civil commotions for many centuries?

To find answers to such questions involved many arduous hours of research into ancient Greek inscriptions and into several brief but enigmatic texts from Rudolf Steiner. One of these texts was hand written from his sick bed, just weeks before he died, the words are hard to decipher, being scribbled onto a notepad.

Part One of this book gives you a clear presentation of Rudolf Steiner's research into the Ephesian Mysteries.

Part Two provides the academically rigorous basis underlying my interpretation of the ancient Greek references to Artemis, and also detailed assessment of some difficult, ambiguous parts of Rudolf Steiner's texts.

It is my hope that this book will answer questions that you have felt about what happened in the Mysteries of Ephesos.

PART ONE

Introduction
The historical, cultural and religious background

The ancient site of Ephesos was situated on the west coast of present-day Turkey. It was one of the greatest sacred sites in the ancient world, functioning for about 1,000 years. The Mysteries here offered acolytes the possibility to enter an initiation process with a focus on contemplating the astral and etheric influences which sustain the life of the Earth. It also provided a pathway to experiencing the process whereby an incarnating soul gained its etheric body. This contemplating of the influences sustaining the Earth and bringing souls into incarnation occurred within what is called the "Moon-sphere". This word simply means the area extending from above the Earth's atmosphere up to the height of the moon, or more precisely, its orbital path around the planet.

The primary deity of these Mysteries was known as Artemis, and later as Diana. From Rudolf Steiner's teachings it is known that at Ephesos, the initiation process involved an acolyte being assisted by the goddess Artemis. This allowed the acolytes to experience, and to integrate, their own spiritual potential: a potential which was nurtured by other spiritual influences in the Moon-sphere.

So a primary focus of the Ephesian Mysteries was a spirit being whom the high priests and priestesses perceived as manifesting, indeed possessing, the essence of the human being's own Higher-self. But in addition, the initiates at Ephesos experienced the thoughts and powerful creative forces of various deities, resonating through the cosmos. In the words of Rudolf Steiner, "this was the site of distinguished academies".[1]

---

[1] GA 243, 4th lect. 14th Aug. 1924.

Relationship with the Christian church

As will be discussed later, some key terms of the Ephesian Mysteries are found in Biblical texts. But there is only one brief historical interaction with the Artemis Mysteries noted in the Bible. This arose from the presence of St. Paul, the Christian missionary when he was at Ephesos in about AD 55. Writing in the Book of Acts, St. Luke reports on the effect of the missionary work undertaken there by St. Paul. We learn that Paul was at Ephesos in the second half of the first century, as part of his missionary journeys in lands around the Mediterranean Sea.

A rumour spread at Ephesos that Paul was somehow undermining, or insulting, the cult of Artemis, with his gospel message. As a result, an angry crowd gathered in the market place, and such was their indignation that for two hours, people shouted, "Great is Diana of the Ephesians".[2]

The situation generally regarding the early years of Christianity and the Mysteries of various cultures, is that the Christian missionaries had the task of spreading the message about the teachings and sacrificial death of Jesus, to the general populace. This was the major social goal of these early missionaries. Any endeavour to establish an esoteric initiatory schooling was a more discreet goal, intended only for the few. Such schooling, about which we have only a few indications, did not seek to establish a new form of the Mysteries; it did not wish to directly rival the long-established Mysteries, such as that of Artemis or of Mithra, Serapis, Athena and Isis.

The primary task of these first missionaries was to awaken the populace to the Gospel message. So, whatever the hierophants in the Mystery centres were achieving, was not relevant to their work. It would

---

[2] Book of Acts 19:28.

have been a mistake for them to associate themselves with the Mysteries.

Moreover, some of the Mysteries were becoming debased, whilst others were struggling to achieve the initiatory processes to they were dedicated.[3] Some were using esoteric techniques which would soon become obsolete, or no longer usable in a changing world. Their time was ebbing away, and as the Christian church gained political ascendency, it shut downs the various Mystery Centres. For amongst the various nations who would be exposed to the Christian message, the old ways of becoming initiated would soon die out, and a humanistic view of life was pre-destined to develop.

For the next two millennia, the message of the Gospels would be widely spread, as a religion without a public initiatory component. It would not be until the modern era that a new approach to the Mysteries would be attempted. The task of Rudolf Steiner was to reveal a new, contemporary pathway to re-establishing the Mysteries.

We shall be exploring here the revelations from Rudolf Steiner regarding the Mysteries at Ephesos. His comments are referring to a time many centuries before the Christian era, when such Mysteries were deeply valid and guided by holy persons, whose strivings were in full alignment with what today we could call the Christ-impulse. For the central being in many of these cults, was in fact an aspect of Christ, or a being who was Christ-aligned, before the descent to Jesus to the Earth.

The site at Ephesos
Although commonly spelt 'Ephesus', this is the traditional Latinized spelling, but this detour through the Latin language is now irrelevant; 'Ephesos' is correct to the Greek spelling. This ancient sacred site

---

[3] GA 237, lect. Aug. 1st, 1924.

is near the present-day Turkish town of Selçuk. Archaeological research has established that there was a town here long before Grecian civilisation arose. It was at some time in the Bronze Age that people settled in this area.

Later, at about the time of Homer (750 BC) a temple was constructed here to serve a cultic purpose. This temple had four sides formed out of four series of columns, and it sheltered a number of sacred artworks. The temple was destroyed by floods, not long after its construction.

In its ruins, archaeologists found a depiction of a griffin, and also a 'Tree of Life'; a cultic symbol of branches of a tree, equally divided on the left and the right sides of the stem. A griffin is an astral form composed from the body of a lion and the wings of an eagle. Its esoteric meaning is not known, but it may refer to the interaction between influences from the astral body and the etheric body. The Tree of Life is generally a representation of the various spiritual realms and astral or etheric energies in the cosmos. The presence of these symbols indicate that esoteric knowledge was a core feature of the rituals there.

Archaeologists have discovered that the temple was re-built several times over the centuries.[4] It is significant that despite the site being prone to flooding it continued to be used over many centuries. This tells us that the clairvoyance of the ancient priests perceived that a spiritual influence was present in that site, a factor which made it an important place, despite its exposure to floods.

The Artemis Mysteries pre-date the time of the Greeks, commencing about 900 BC and continuing for some time into the Christian era. Very little is known academically about these Mysteries, or the true

---

[4] D.G. Hogarth, "*The archaic Artemisia of Ephesus*" London, 1908.

nature of the goddess Artemis or Diana. It has nothing to do with the popular cult figure of Artemis, who was associated with flora and fauna, and with healing and fertility. The Romans later merged the cult of Artemis with that of their own nature-goddess, known as Diana. Our primary source of knowledge of the Mysteries of antiquity, whether of Artemis, or Isis or other deities, is from the spiritual-scientific research of Rudolf Steiner.

Academic research can point out various primitive rituals or popular customs concerning Artemis-Diana. But all of this is irrelevant to the esoteric initiatory activity experienced in the Mysteries. To summarize what Rudolf Steiner taught, one can conclude that in the resonating presence of the goddess Artemis, the acolyte experienced the matrix of their own eternal, cosmic self.

The rituals of the Mysteries of Ephesos continued to be celebrated in the last, and truly magnificent temple, which had been erected after the previous building was destroyed. The previous temple had a wooden frame, making it vulnerable to fire; it was destroyed by an arsonist in 356 BC. The work on this new building began in 323 BC; it was 450 ft (137m) long, 225 ft (69m) wide and 60 ft (18m) high, with more than 127 columns. It was constructed of marble, and adorned with paintings, and its columns were gilded in gold and silver.

It was double the size of the Parthenon; its size and artistic magnificence earned it the epithet, "The Seventh Wonder of the World". The temple was damaged in 268 AD by invading Goths, but continued in use until about 407AD. This is when the Christian church authorities forcibly closed all the sites of the Mysteries.

Long before the Christian era, for many centuries, so deeply revered was Artemis, that the temple dedicated to her was regarded as inviolate. The powerful Persian war-lord Xerxes, spared it alone of all the religious building of Greece, and also Caesar Augustus refrained from destroying it.

Chapter One
An over-view of Rudolf Steiner's teachings
The statue of Artemis

The actual experiences that the acolytes underwent in the initiation procedures enacted there were kept secret. Secrecy about the initiation process was strictly maintained at every initiatory site in the ancient world. Hence scholarly research can say very little about Artemis or about the inner reality of the Ephesian Mysteries. There are only brief references in to these inner processes in ancient Greek texts, and these references are inconsistent and vague.

There are also only two or three lectures in the Complete Works of Rudolf Steiner where Artemis is mentioned. But there are also some entries in private notes of Rudolf Steiner's about Ephesos, together with two verses written for one of his students, Dr. Ita Wegman (1876-1948), a Dutch doctor who was a member of the Executive of the Anthroposophical Society, and was leader of the Medical Section of the Anthroposophical Society; she devoted her life to the nurturing of anthroposophical medicine.

In recent decades, these brief texts have been published, providing vital information about this site.[5] When all these various documents are contemplated, with knowledge of the ancient Greek language, and the esoteric basis of Greek mythology, it becomes possible to uncover some inspiring secrets of the initiation experiences at Ephesos.

It may be a helpful if we start by summarizing the preliminary points as indicated in these various documents from Rudolf Steiner. We also note that

---

[5] Some texts are private notebook entries, made available by the Rudolf Steiner Archives; others were published in a book about Ita Wegman, by M. and E. Kirchner-Bockhol: *Rudolf Steiner's Mission and Ita Wegman*, London, 1977.

Rudolf Steiner used the version 'Ephesus', which was customary a century ago.

* This name 'Artemis' is a popular exoteric term for a deity (but Rudolf Steiner does not reveal the esoteric name for this deity).

 * The features of the rituals were designed to bring the acolytes into a perception of the etheric realms, amongst other experiences.

* The acolytes at Ephesos could learn much about the spiritual forces behind human speech.

* Artemis is the same deity (or same personification of spiritual influences) as Diana.

* Artemis-Diana is a lunar being (or more accurately, a personification of) lunar spiritual influences.[6]

* The Mysteries of Artemis-Diana unveiled the connection of the human being with the spiritual realms.[7]

* The cult of Artemis was inherently linked with the Mysteries of Demeter and Persephone. These were especially celebrated at Eleusis in Greece.

* A little-known deity called 'Mysa', representing the Spiritual-self, was an important deity in the Artemis Mysteries.

* The group of letters, 'Hieraos', provide a key to the secret initiation experience of these Mysteries.

* Various documents from Rudolf Steiner imply that the famous god Dionysos, as well as a mysterious deity called Iackhos, are both part of the spiritual

---

[6] GA 246 p. 74.
[7] GA 126 p.18.

context of the Mysteries at Ephesos. (The nature and significance of these two deities are explained below.)

We can now begin to explore what the initiate Rudolf Steiner has revealed about the spiritual experiences and intentions of the Ephesian Mysteries. We will start with his comments about the statute of Artemis.

The statue of Artemis
The great temple of Artemis at Ephesus housed the famous statue of Artemis, with many breasts (see illustration 1). This feature is identifying Artemis as representing the etheric and astral influences which sustain the life and fertility of the Earth. As Rudolf Steiner explained,

> In the centre of the Ephesian Mysteries was a statue of the goddess, Artemis. This statue of a feminine figure with many breasts may today have a grotesque quality, but this is only because the modern viewer has no intuition as to how such artworks were experienced in olden times. In the past the actual experience of such imagery was a central feature of the spiritual process.
>
> The acolytes of the Mysteries had to undergo various preparatory stages, through which they were guided to the actual centre of the Mysteries. The central feature of the Ephesian Mysteries architecturally was this statue of Artemis. When the acolyte was led to this central image, they became one with such an image. In that the person stood before the statue, he or she ceased to have consciousness of existing within their skin.
>
> Instead the acolyte began to feel their consciousness merging with what this statue is. They identified themselves with the statue. And this identifying oneself with the statue had the result that one no longer gazed out to the earthly realms: to stones, trees, rivers,

clouds and so on. Instead, through this feeling of oneself as being one with the image of Artemis, perceptions of one's connection with the ether-world were inwardly received.

The acolyte felt as if merging with the starry realms, with processes occurring amongst the planets and the stars. She or he no longer felt the earthly substantiality within the human skin, but instead felt as if in a cosmic existence. They felt as if now existing in the etheric.[8]

The statue and speech (the Logos)
Rudolf Steiner's further comments on this are,

In Ephesos the student was led before a statue, a statue known as a depiction of Artemis. And in that the student identified with this statue, which was full of life, which rayed out life, the student's consciousness lived into the cosmic ether. The student was raised right out of the inner experience or feeling of simply terrestrial existence, and was raised up into the experiencing of the cosmic ether.

In this experience, there was conveyed firstly to the student what human speech is. Then regarding human speech, the acolyte realized: human speech is a reflected-image of (*cosmic*) speech – speech is a 'human logos', a reflection of the 'cosmic Logos' or cosmic Word. To the acolyte it was conveyed how the cosmic Word, from which human speech derives, creatively surges and moves through the cosmos.[9]

The Mystery Centre of Ephesos
In the following extract from a lecture by Rudolf Steiner, we are given a description of the spiritual

---

[8] GA 233, lect. 26th Dec. 1923
[9] GA 233 lect. 27th Dec. 1923

'atmosphere' in which the acolytes at Ephesos were living.

Associated with the rites of Initiation, conversations between teachers and pupils often took place in the evening twilight, as they walked along quiet woodland paths. These conversations prepared the soul for genuine experiences of the Nature-processes during their sleep at night. The candidate first experienced in Ephesus, the mystery of the Word and the rites connected with the worship of Diana.

Then rites were carried out, whereby the candidate for initiation was introduced to the secrets of macrocosmic evolution. The secrets of nature were then expounded to him or her with graphic vividness in distinguished Academies of learning. It was in the surrounding nature that the conversations associated with these rites took place.

As already described, the sea reached the actual steps of the ceremonial buildings, which were surrounded by silent groves. It was in this environment that the instruction and the conversations took place between the teacher and the pupil. The gaze of the Initiate was open into the spiritual realms and he or she was fully conscious of the creative, form-giving, activity of spiritual beings working with consummate wisdom from the zodiac and planetary spheres.

The teacher spoke of the ever-creative Spirit holding sway eternally – an experience resulting from his or her Initiation in an illuminated sleep-consciousness. The teacher spoke of the form-giving forces, of Spiritus Mundi {*the 'Soul of the World'*}. Through these teachings, the teacher developed in the pupil a deepened view of nature which resulted in their sleep becoming rich in inner experiences. The teacher spoke words such as these:

> "Look upon your human form in its totality. Beneath our feet are the plants and around us are the lengthening shadows of twilight and the dim green hue of the temple grove. The

first stars are beginning to twinkle in the heavens. Behold the majesty and grandeur, but also the budding and sprouting of life in the Heavens above and the Earth beneath. And then behold yourself."

After such instruction, sleep was not the same as before, but teemed with inner experiences. The pupil could penetrate into the realm of the elemental beings working in warmth, air, water and earth. In a state of 'waking sleep-consciousness' he or she perceived how these (*nature-*)beings loosen and crumble earthly matter, thus making room for the roots of the plants and at the same time enabling them to consolidate their own form.

The acolyte also perceived how these beings everywhere keep the watery element in movement, thus enabling the saps to stream upwards in opposition to the force of gravity, and how they are active in every manifestation of the elements of air and warmth. And behind these elements, the pupil was conscious of Persephone (*or Ceres*), the daughter of Demeter, actively present as the non-material foundation of all substance; to this 'Goddess' all the elements are obedient.

Thus during sleep, the pupil could become conscious of matter (*as something which is*) permeated by spirit, (*and thus*) of the great primal **Mother of the World,** of the 'Mater-alma'. Thus the pupil could bring to the Teacher who was himself or herself, indirectly conscious of the "Spiritus Mundi", knowledge of what is a direct, active influence on Earth, as a "speculum spiritus mundi {*a mirror of the World Spirit*}".[10]

Commentary:
From this lecture extract, we see how the acolytes were able to perceive the ethers, and thus the energies and spirit beings within the etheric fields

---

[10] From GA 243, 4th lect. 14th Aug. 1924.

that sustain the Earth, which are primarily directed from the Moon. All of this is meant by the name Artemis, or Diana. But we also note that once an acolyte is in such an experience, then the realm of Persephone (also called Proserpina or Ceres) is encountered.

This in turn means that these energies and beings are experienced as the foundation of the living Earth. Rudolf Steiner once commented that Persephone is the spiritual basis behind living Nature.[11] So 'Persephone' is a personification of a number of spiritual forces which help sustain the Earth. From this experience, it is just one step further to experience the realm of Demeter, the "World-Mother". In other words, the initiate became aware of the spiritual matrix of our human consciousness. But from the perspective of regarding human souls as being children of the Earth. In Rudolf Steiner words,

> Demeter is the representative of that being, from which human consciousness has derived...but Demeter is (*here understood as*) the kind of spirit being which arises from the spiritual forces belonging to the Earth. Thus Demeter is the primal being of the Earth...and (*also*) a being who wills to bestow immortality upon the human being.

Rudolf Steiner continues, saying of Demeter that,

> "She is the divine creator of the eternal spirit in the human being; the cause of the clairvoyantly enlightened consciousness, and

---

[11] Regarding Persephone or Proserpina Rudolf Steiner also gave two other interpretations:
 A: GA 129, p.17: Persephone is the old, still clairvoyantly aware human soul.
 B: GA 180, p. 105: Persephone is the human soul, which has to descend into incarnation in the darkened world of matter.

she is from the same tapestry of divine
energies as those which created the Earth..." [12]

A personal glimpse of ancient Ephesos
Very brief notes of the more intimate personal,
experience of the acolyte at Ephesos exist in Rudolf
Steiner Archives. I have expanded these brief notes
are into a readable narrative; they are in effect, saying
this:

> It is late in the day; the landscape is
> enshrouded in darkness. Buildings with
> angular forms are perceptible all around. Two
> human figures walk across the scene towards
> the trees which loom, darkly green and almost
> black in the already late twilight. Other figures
> follow these two, coming from various
> directions; all of them walking towards the
> woods. There are many paths through the
> shrubs and trees, all of which lead into a
> rather narrower path surrounded by dense
> undergrowth. Along this narrow avenue the
> walkers are approaching the Temple of the
> Goddess Artemis, at Ephesos.

> It is now evening; the countryside around is
> shrouded in darkness. The Moon is rising
> above the horizon, the conversations between
> the walkers are gradually silenced, and in a
> mood of earnestness and contemplation the
> figures approach the steps to the Temple door.
> With a certain rhythm which is repeated three
> times, they knock on the Temple door.

> The door is opened for those seeking entrance,
> a faint ray of light illumines the entrance to
> the Temple, a light which radiates from the
> One[13] who has opened the gate. "Who are
> you?" asks the being whose form is not sharply

---

[12] GA 8, p.95 and in GA 34, p.155, Persephone is called the
Earth-soul.
[13] This being is a kind of Guardian of the Threshold figure.

outlined, but from whom this light is radiating. (*A dialogue then ensues.*)

"We are kinspeople and known to you of old."

"You are Earth-persons, unfaithful; you have forgotten your ancient and primeval Guardian.

"We have gathered fruits in earthly life for Eternity."

Before your fruits, my light vanishes away."

"I will hold this light for as long as we may need it."

Thus, with a certain gesture, speaks the voice of one of the first two figures. He is the leader. They all go forward and the light continues to help them illumine their steps. . . After a while they stand before the image of the Goddess Artemis, placed at the east end of the Temple.

"Take hold of what stands before you", speaks the voice of the leader.

The light is now extinguished, darkness reigns and the moonlight coming from above, gradually illumines the image of the Goddess. [14]

We can regret that Rudolf Steiner did not write down some further points about this scene inside the magnificent temple, upon which we could expand, to fashion further inspiring narratives.

---

[14] This narrative was produced by this author from Rudolf Steiner's brief notes, published in GA 243, p.234.

Chapter Two

Artemis and Speech: IOA

The next lecture extract we shall consider presents a description of the experience of speech by the acolytes at Ephesos, especially the three key vowels, I,A,O. These three vowels, I,O,A were also used as a sacred name of the Divine by the Greek Gnostics. But it is significant that these vowels are also core vowels in names of some prominent men in the Gospels; those named 'John'. For in Greek, John is *Ioann*: this name consists primarily of these three vowels A,I,O (plus two 'n's).

It is very striking that here in this lecture we already encounter a cosmopolitan view of Christianity, a view which transcends traditional boundaries. The IAO is an integral part of the Ephesian Mysteries, and yet it is also inherent in Greek Gnostic texts.

There is firstly, John the Baptist; and in the Greek text of the Gospel, this fact of his name being 'John' is especially emphasised: "There was begotten a man, sent forth from God, his name: 'John'" [15] That is, the Greek text simply says, "...*his name: John*". But the sentence here could have been: "...the name given to him was, John the Baptist". But it only says abruptly, "John", as if to emphasize this name. This name is significant in early Christian texts; there is Lazaros who, Rudolf Steiner reports, was given the 'Mystery name' John, after his initiation experience of being awakened out of death, by Jesus himself.

Rudolf Steiner taught that his Gospel is called the Gospel of John, showing how significant was this mystery name to Lazaros. Various theologians now

---

[14] In the Greek: onoma auto Ioannaes :
ὄνομα αὐτῷ ᾿Ιωάννης·.

attribute the authorship of this Gospel to Lazaros.[16] There is also Mark, the young friend of St. Peter, who wrote the Gospel of St. Mark. He is several times referred to as, "John Mark". But more striking is the giving of the name 'John' to St. Peter, by Jesus. This occurs at crucial occasions in the interaction between Jesus and St. Peter.

When Peter is first brought to meet Jesus, by his brother Andrew, Jesus declares, "You are Simon, son of John...". Another occasion occurred at that holy moment when the risen Jesus becomes perceptible to the Disciples higher, visionary capacity. Jesus then refers to St. Peter as, "Peter, son of John..."

These may be viewed as 'ritual' re-namings, intended to reveal and affirm his spiritual success or primary life-challenge on his apostolic path. It is most unlikely that they are due to Jesus wanting to formally stipulate the name of Peter's father, precisely at the moment when Peter's own specific 'ego' or selfhood is facing a major challenge.

Spiritually informed contemplation on the verses concludes that such a legalistic and blood-lineage motivation is fully irrelevant to, and also deeply alien to, the view of Jesus on familial connections when it comes to taking up the esoteric Christian Path. You have to be following Him without putting major emphasis on blood-lineage and family connections.

These 're-namings' occurred when Peter was facing intense spiritual challenges occurring on these two occasions (see at Jhn. 1:42 and 21:15-17). The third example where St. Peter is re-named, is in St. Matthew's Gospel (see at Matt.16:17). So the fact that the Baptist was to be named 'John' is an indicator

---

[16] For example, V. Eller, *The Beloved Disciple*, B. Eerdmans, 1987, and many others in Church conferences and Journals.

that his soul had divine influences and qualities within it.

It is relevant here to note that these three vowels are referred to by some ancient writers, as being the name of God to the Hebrew priests; even though this is not what those priests would have specifically acknowledged. For example, the ancient Greek historian, Diodorus Siculus, writing in 384 AD (*Works 1:94*), stated that, "The Jews ascribed his (Moses) laws (*i.e., the 10 Commandments*) as being derived from the God who is invoked as "IOA".

Flavius Clement of Alexandria also indicates this same view, in his *Stromata* (*V.6:34*), where he states that the high priests at the Jewish temple were called "Iaou" (Ιαού). And later, the 5th century Greek theologian Theodoret, states that the title for people working as adjunct helpers in the Jewish Temple, "...were referred to as 'Nethinim' which means 'gift of IAO'."[17] This appears to be his unique interpretation, as the common understanding of this term is, "those given (or set apart) as servants".

But Theodoret's text confirms an ancient understanding that the vowels IAO are in some way the name of the Divine One. In fact, evidence is emerging this was also the understanding of the early Christians, as documents from the first centuries of the church show that many people did at times refer to 'God' as IAO.[18]

If this closeness between the New Testament and the apparently quite separate religion or Mystery wisdom of Artemis is not surprising enough, to the readers' astonishment in this same lecture, Rudolf Steiner moves into the theme of a sacred name experienced by Ephesian initiates. This name is 'Jehovah', sacred

---

[17] Bishop Theodoret, (423-457) in *Quaest in 1*. Paral., section 9.
[18] A.Hylton: *Kurios, Tetragrammaton, IAO among Jews, Gnostics and the early church.*

to the Hebrew religion. It is significant that this word has these same three vowels as its core, plus several consonants.

Yet this remarkable cultural or religious inter-connectedness is not mentioned at all by Rudolf Steiner in his lecture. (We shall explore the origin of the name Jehovah, below.) There now follows a long extract from the lecture where this theme of the I,A,O is presented, as well as the origin of the name 'Jehovah'. This lecture also includes a very significant astrological verse,

> ....Now, if one wants to gain perception as to how the human being, by means of the lunar energies, has its radiant ether-body bestowed upon it, then a person can observe this. It can be observed by lunar observations: I could even say, by means of the 'spiritual Moon Observatory', one sees how these ether energies are transferred to the human being.

> To do this, to rightly understand how this occurs....it is important to let one's feelings and mind be influenced by the role of human beings in such a cosmic truth; for people were directly involved in this process over the Ages.

> In fact, the involvement of human souls in this descent from pre-earthly existence was never so subtly, so intimately, perceived as that which occurred in the Mysteries of Ephesos. That is, in regard to the providing the human being with its enveloping sheath; its etheric body.

> In the Mysteries of Ephesos it was the case that the entirety of the rituals and offerings which were brought to the goddess of Ephesos, exoterically called 'Artemis', were in fact intended to bring about an experiencing of the vibrant spiritual activity occurring in the world's ether.

One can indeed say that, when those souls belonging to the Mystery of Ephesos approached the image of the deity, they then had a feeling, a feeling which intensified to an inner hearing. This inner hearing could be described as if the goddess herself was speaking: 'I rejoice in all that capacity - which is spread throughout the cosmic ether - which sustains (*earthly*) fertility.'

This declaring of an inner joy of the temple's goddess about all that which growing, sprouting, blossoming in the far reaches of the cosmic ether, made a deep impression.

It was in particular this inner empathy with the sprouting and growing of new buds which permeated the atmosphere, the spiritual atmosphere around the sanctuary, giving it an enchanted mood.

The elements of this Mystery were so arranged that one can say that nowhere else was the growth of the plants, within the sprouting and growing capacity of the Earth within the plant world, so vividly experienced than at Ephesos.

This then also had the result that precisely in the Ephesian Mystery, (esoteric) instructions could be given with particular clarity. The instruction there, if I can call it that, was especially focussed on this Moon secret, about which I spoke yesterday. This was a secret which the teachings there sought to bring close to the souls of those who were participating.

This secret was something which everyone there had as their own experience; that is, to feel oneself as a 'form of light'. This could happen because the process of acquiring one's 'form of light' (*the ether body*) from the Moon (*the ethers in the lunar sphere*) was so livingly portrayed to the students and to those already initiated.

There was also an arrangement in Ephesos which was like the following. A person who was able to let this initiatory procedure have a real impact them, was actually brought fully into the process through which the etheric body is formed by the sunlight. (The sunlight which changes the form of the Moon's disk).[19]

Then there resounded across to this student, (*in the Moon-sphere*) as if resounding over to them from the Sun:
I O A. This I O A – of which the student knew it vivified his or her astral body.
So, I O – the ego or 'I' and the astral body;
then the approach of the radiant ether-body in the A;
and thus together: I O A.
So, now the acolyte, because in their soul the 'I O A' was vibrating, felt themselves as I, as astral body, and as etheric body.

And then, it was as if from the Earth there resounded upwards – for the acolyte was now transferred up into cosmic reality – as if up from the Earth, there resounded that which permeated these I O A sounds. These ascending sounds were the terrestrial forces; they rose up to the inner hearing as "eh-v".

So now one felt oneself within the IehOvAh (*i.e., Jehovah*); the full human being felt itself within this (combination of three vowels and consonants). This experience was an anticipatory feeling, through these consonants,

---

[19] This sentence is somewhat obscure; it appears to refer to the changing shape of the Moon (from a crescent through to a full disc) as being due, from an Earth-dweller's perspective, to the amount of sunlight shining upon it.

of the physical body, which the person seeking incarnation would have only when incarnated.

These are consonants which belong together with those vowels – I O A – which allude to the I, the astral body and the etheric body. This living into the 'Jehovah' was what the student at Ephesos could dimly feel as the last step of the descent down out of the spiritual realm.

But at the same time, this dim inner feeling of the I O A was such that one felt oneself existing within the light as this same resonance: I O A. In this way, one was a human being: resonating I, resonating astral body, within the radiant, glowing etheric body. Then one became Resonance in the Light. Such is the human being, as a cosmic human being.

Thereby one is able to take up into one's soul that which one sees out there in the cosmos. Just as here on the Earth one is able to take up into one's soul what happens in the physical world around us.

When this happened, the Ephesian student, when they carried within their soul this I O A , really felt as if transferred up into the Moon-sphere. Such an acolyte took part in what could be observed from the perspective of the Moon. There the (incarnating) human being was still a human being in the general (non-gender) sense.

The person first becomes man or woman as they descend closer to the Earth (anticipating conception). There the human being felt itself as transferred up into this region of the pre-earthy existence, but one sensed in fact the approach of the earthly.

For the Ephesian student, this being taken up into the Moon-sphere was actually possible in an especially close, intimate manner. Then they carried in their hearts, in their souls, that which they had experienced, which resounded to the acolytes of Ephesos in this way:

Offspring of the cosmos !
Thou in a form of light,
Empowered by the Sun, in the Moon's might:
On thee was bestowed the
creative resonating of Mars
and Mercury's limb-stirring whirling motion.
Illumined wert thou by
Jupiter's shining wisdom,
and the love-bearing beauty of Venus,
So that Saturn's primeval Spirit-inwardness
may consecrate thee to the
realm of space and the flow of time !

It was this which permeated (*the soul of*) every Ephesian (*acolyte*); and this (*cosmic aspect of the soul*) is what he or she valued as belonging to the most important thing that pulsed through their human nature.[20] As Rudolf Steiner commented on another occasion, "Many students of the Mysteries at Ephesos gazed at the earthly reality, from the ether."[21]

The German original of the above verse,

Weltentsprossenes Wesen, du in Lichtgestalt,
Von der Sonne erkraftet in der Mondgewalt,
Dich beschenket des Mars erschaffendes Klingen
Und Merkurs gliedbewegende Schwingen,
Dich erleuchtet Jupiters erstrahlende Weisheit
Und der Venus liebetragende Schönheit
Daß Saturns weltenalte Geist-Innigkeit
Dich dem Raumessein und
Zeitenwerden weihe !

---

[20] GA 233A, lect. 22nd April 1924.
[21] GA 233, lect. 31st Dec. 1923.

Contemplating this 'Astrology' verse from Ephesos
From this lecture extract, we see that when Rudolf
Steiner refers to the Mysteries at Ephesos as giving
perception into the ethers to the acolytes and
initiates. This means that these people had, as a
major focus, the spiritual processes whereby the
human soul becomes incarnate. It also means that the
Ephesian Mysteries resulted in substantial experience
of what we call astrology, or the influence of the
planets on our astral body. We shall now explore this
verse, starting with these lines:

> Offspring of the cosmos,
> thou in a form of light,
> Empowered by the Sun,
> in the Moon's might:

These lines are declaring that the Ephesian initiates
were beholding the soul or astral body, as it descends
into the Moon-sphere. At this stage the human being
has an astral body, but shortly after descending into
the Moon-sphere, an etheric body is also formed for
this person. This process takes only a few seconds, as
the four ethers stream into a common point, forming
a new etheric body.[22] The inherent virtues and
impediments of the incarnating soul are determined
by the karma of that person. This karmic outcome is
the result of the many centuries that the soul has
spent in spiritual realms after its previous life. The
deeper-seated, longer-term attitude and feelings of
the soul in a past life, living on within the astral body,
determine many qualities existing in the etheric body
of the next incarnation.

This new etheric body is a radiant object ("in a form
of light"), and has its origin from the Sun-sphere
("empowered by the Sun"). All our etheric forces have
their origin from the vast and radiant ether-body of
the Sun. But once the etheric body is created, the
Moon has a strong influence over its dynamics ("in

---

[22] GA 100, lect. 21st June 1907

the Moon's might"), especially the capacity for fertility.

The next line in the verse,

> On thee was bestowed the creative resonating
> of Mars,

refers to the inherent capacity of Mars to empower our astral nature, our soul. Rudolf Steiner taught that Mars is the force behind the intensity of our inner life; whether thinking, feeling or will.[23] It creates the vehemence which becomes the energy behind our actions, and hence our creativity.

Regarding the next line,

> and Mercury's limb-stirring whirling motion

it is significant that it speaks of the impact of Mercury on the physical body, rather than on the soul (astral body), as the verse did with regard to Mars. Rudolf Steiner speaks of Mercury forces being so predominant in a kindergarten, because these energies are naturally predominant in young children there. The children are inwardly impelled as a result of the Mercury influences, to run around and skip and play. They are also impelled to add the vowel 'i', to the name of anything which pleases them; thus Tom becomes 'Tommy'. This vowel in English is often written as 'ee', (not 'ei'). This vowel is the expression of Mercury influences. The next line,

> Illumined wert thou by Jupiter's shining wisdom...

reflects an experience of the Ephesian initiates which is affirmed by anthroposophical wisdom and classical astrology. Namely, if wisdom is a quality in the soul, then this shows in the horoscope and in the aura as a strong presence of noble Jupiter influences. Rudolf Steiner taught that wisdom, meaning here intuitive higher thinking, creates the 'spiritual-soul', and that

---

[23] GA 213, lect, 1st July 1922.

these qualities ray into us from Jupiter. He consequently gave the hierarchical spirits in the Jupiter sphere the name, "the Spirits of Wisdom"; and taught that these beings help our soul, when we are asleep, to receive wisdom, as it passes through the Jupiter sphere.[24]

The following line is,

> and the love-bearing beauty of Venus

The influence of Venus is well known astrologically to create beauty in a person's appearance, as well as imbuing the soul with a capacity for the arts. A person with positive Venus influences has an interest in, and usually the capacity for, creating beautiful objects, and therefore an artistic gift. Such qualities in a person cause others to have romantic love feelings for this person.

But in this line, we also see that the Ephesian initiates perceived how still higher spiritual influences from Venus can bestow divine qualities on a person; namely, the actual 'spirit', which Rudolf Steiner calls the 'Spiritual-self' (see the Glossary for a brief explanation of such anthroposophical terms.)

This arises when the astral nature is very substantially purified and refined. Such a quality as the Spiritual-self invokes love for that person from others, a love which is called 'agape'. That is, not romantic affection, but a deep love which includes the will, not only the emotions. In addition, people who have spirituality, in this deeper sense, also find that they experience love (agape) for all creatures. So the phrase, 'love-bearing beauty' has several deep meanings.

The last lines are,

---

[24] GA 228, lect. 27.July, 1923.

So that Saturn's primeval Spirit-inwardness
might consecrate thee to
the realm of space and the flow of time !

These lines reflect the awareness of the Ephesian priestesses and priests, that the influence of Saturn in the soul has the potential to be of vital importance. If the higher influences from the majestic and stern deities of the Saturn sphere, known as the Thrones, can be cognized by the human being, this can allow some awareness as to what are her or his real karmic life-priorities.

These intuitive insights ray up from the deeper, less conscious, layers of the soul. These insights indicate to us what is the best course of action we could undertake to meet our karmic obligations. This influence from Saturn is possible because the sublime Thrones, in the Saturn sphere, accurately and loyally keep awareness of humanity's karma. As Rudolf Steiner taught in another lecture, they are connected with,

> "...the deepest inner-reality of our solar system; this is something similar to our own remembering of what is our deepest inner soul-life on the Earth...the Thrones keep in their memory, knowledge of all that happens in our solar system, and are connected to the eternal Higher-self of each human being."[25]

Should this high intuitive wisdom be heard as a still, inner voice in the soul, then that person's incarnation can really be 'consecrated' to the spatial world where time prevails, for such a person dedicates themselves to a life which evolves their spiritual potential, to assist uplifting the over-all karma of humanity.

We noted earlier the blurring of the boundaries between religions, in that the Ephesian Mysteries had an inner link to IOA and thus to the Biblical use of the

---

[25] GA 228, lect. 2nd Sept, 1923.

name 'John' and also to the sacred Biblical name of Jehovah.

We now need to consider the origin of the name 'Jehovah'. Scholars are not able to clearly determine the origin of this name. Many contradictory statements are therefore made about this word. Some sources declare that it first appeared in 1381 AD. Other sources state that it first appeared in 1520, in the Tyndale Bible. But neither viewpoint is really meaningful, because people such as Tyndale were simply attempting to render a much older, medieval Hebrew name for God, that is, 'JHVH', into English.

The medieval Jewish version, with the vowels from the word Adonai, appears from editorial work in the Hebrew Scriptures, undertaken by 'Masoretic' scholars. But it appears likely that already in the early Hellenistic Age, Jewish people were incorporating the vowels IAO with the consonants JHVH, to create a word to refer to God; a word which was similar to 'Jehovah'.

This Masoretic term itself was an attempt by 8th century Hebrew scholars, to adopt a name that would indicate a sacred meaning, belonging to the four letters used as a name for God in their Scriptures already in Genesis: JHVH, whilst respecting that people were forbidden to pronounce the name of God.

Rudolf Steiner's research has particularly strong support from some modern scholars, who have concluded that the name 'Jehovah' actually has no specific origin in language, "it is meaningless, in an etymological sense".[26] That is, with regard to etymology, i.e., the study of origin of the words, this word has no antecedents or earlier words from which

---

[26] MacLaurin, E.C.B. "*YHWH the Origin of the Tetra-grammaton.*" Vetus Testamentum, vol. 12, no.4, 1962, pp.439-463. JSTOR.www.jstor.org/stable/1526934.Accessed 12. Jan. 2021.

it may derive. So how was it formed? Rudolf Steiner has made an extraordinary contribution to this theme, when he reveals that the resonance of vowels and consonants, inwardly heard within the ether, by initiates in Ephesos, resulted in the forming of the name, Jehovah.

Whether this experience at Ephesos was transferred across to the Hebrew priesthood, or whether they had their own experience of these cosmic influences, is unknown. But there is also another fascinating cross-over point between the Ephesian cult and Biblical religiosity; namely the Essenes.

The Essenes

In our contemplation of the Artemis Mysteries, we need to explore this truly striking cultural-religious interconnection. The first point to note is that a particular class of priests at Ephesos were actually called "the Essenes".[27] This is of course exactly the same name as that of the esoteric Hebrew group with their centre at Qumran in Palestine, and whose scriptures were found in the 20th century, which became known as the Dead Sea Scrolls.

Scholars are not sure whether this Greek usage of the word 'Essene' is directly linked to the same Hebrew term, or not. But it is my conclusion, and that of various scholars, that these two, apparently entirely different religions, are indeed using the very same word.

It is known that in Gerasa, Palestine, some centuries before Christianity, a temple dedicated to Artemis existed, which grew in importance, during the era when Palestine was under Roman control[28].

---

[27] E.L. Hicks, *Greek Inscriptions in the British Museum*, 1874, in ancient Greek, Ἐσσῆνες.

[28] John Kampen, *The Cult of Artemis and the Essenes in Syro-Palestine,* in Dead Sea Discoveries, Vol.10, No. 2 (2003) pps. 204-220.

A typically many-breasted statue of Artemis was unearthed there in 1961, and another at Abila in 1994. Remains of temples or shrines dedicated to Artemis have been found throughout the Middle East.

That the priestly Essenes shared a name with one class of priests in the Artemis Mysteries, which is a religion or cult which had its origin in Asia Minor, amongst the pre-Grecian peoples, is remarkable. Rudolf Steiner taught that this word "Essene' derives from a Hebrew term for 'healer'; a statement which found confirmation in 1960, in the research by G. Vermes, the official translator of the Dead Sea scrolls.[29] But we note that in the Dead Sea Scrolls, the word 'healer' meant a person who heals the soul, not the body, and who heals the soul of its spiritual lowliness.

It appears that the name 'Essene' was applied to that particular class of priests in the Artemis Mysteries, about 200-100 BC, and not from earlier centuries, because the Essenes did not exist in earlier times. So there are two possibilities: one is that this same name was applied to the priests of Artemis (in the Hellenistic age only), by the general community, because people were aware of a similar type of function or spiritual philosophy between the two groups.

The other possibility is that there existed a collegial interaction between the two groups, as their spiritual initiatory striving was so similar. This led the Essenes to describe the Artemis priest as in effect, belonging to the same path; so they too, were 'Essenes', that is, soul-healers. Rudolf Steiner does not indicate which of these is the correct conclusion.

---

[29] G. Vermes, *The Etymology of "Essenes"*, in Revue de Qumrân, Vol. 2, No. 3 (7) pp. 427-443, June 1960.

Chapter 3
Meditative texts about Ephesus from Rudolf Steiner

Now we can start to contemplate several of Rudolf Steiner's meditative verses and notebook entries. These were mainly written down during the last year of his life, when, in poor health, he was restricted to a sick-bed.

We shall be exploring these various texts as contemplations on the Mysteries of Ephesos. There are two verses included in which Rudolf Steiner is confirming to a colleague, a member of the Executive of the Anthroposophical Society, Dr. Ita Wegman, that she had been incarnate at Ephesus, as an acolyte, (about 600 BC).[30]

In contrast to this verse, his private notebook entries are about various deities and human soul qualities, and don't refer to a specific acolyte. These notebook writings provide invaluable light on what the initiatory path at Ephesos invoked.

Rudolf Steiner's notebook entries

A 1924 private notebook entry of Rudolf Steiner about the Mysteries at Ephesus.

Rudolf Steiner made two entries in his private notebooks about this theme. In one version, the text has the words 'Artemisia' and 'Isrenum' written above it; another version of the same text has just the word 'Isrenum'. Such notebook entries are brief and were intended for his personal use. I have added some explanatory comments in brackets and in italics, to help clarify the text. The name 'Isrenum' occurs only in this notebook entry, and refers to a spiritual being in the Moon-sphere.

---

[30] M. & E. Kirchner-Bockholt, *Rudolf Steiner's Mission und Ita Wegman*, Rudolf Steiner Press, London, 1977

It is natural to assume that the word Artemisia refers to a festival or sacred rite in which this goddess has a central role; perhaps she appears to the acolytes then. This word appears only two times in the works of Rudolf Steiner, and one assumes that it must have this kind of meaning.

But, as is discussed in Part Two, the word 'Artemisia' appears never to have been used by the ancient Greeks as the name of a sacred festival honouring or involving Artemis. As such it is never included in any Ancient Greek-English dictionaries as having this meaning.

But in the last phase of ancient Greek civilisation, when it was under the control of the Roman Empire, this word was used for some kind of festival by Greek writers who were representing, or being mindful of, the Roman authorities. Yet this usage of the word is not mentioned in such dictionaries. So 'Artemisia' is a tem which is itself an enigma; it appears to be not an ancient Greek word for a sacred festival involving Artemis. (This enigma is explored in Part Two.)

So the question has to arise: just what did Rudolf Steiner mean, when he used this word? In view of the above facts, there is the strong possibility – bearing in mind Rudolf Steiner was ill, only some weeks away from death – that he meant to write 'Artemüsia' not Artemisia. As is discussed below, this alternative word – which is not an actual Greek word – is in fact interwoven within the body of the text. That is, an 'acrostic' is built into the text; the first letters of each line, about half way down, spell the word 'Artemüsia'.[31]

We don't need to focus on the complex initial lines about the interaction of divine hierarchical beings within the head or limbs of the human being. It is in

---

[31] In *Rudolf Steiner's Mission*, by Kirchner-Bockholt, (Ref.5).

the later lines that references to the Ephesian Mysteries occur.

Isrenum   Artemisia*   (*= Artemüsia ?)

> In the 15th to 18th century spiritual School of Michael {*the following was made known to the not yet incarnate souls*:}
> anthroposophy shows itself to be the content of that which arises, because the First Hierarchy in permeating humanity,
> advances to the interior of the head;
> this {*process*} has been made possible through the extrusion of the Moon {*from the Earth*}.
> Previously the human periphery commenced from the head, but now the limb-system of the human being became this
> {*i.e., the starting point of moving out to the periphery*}
> ....this change {*came about*} through a {*specific*} spiritual being, {*called*} "Isrenum", who is especially close to (*Archangel*) Michael and who is the regent of the Moon-cycles
> and {*who*} thereby has
> the possibility of gazing at the cosmos from the most varied aspects (*from the ever-changing motions of the moon*).
>
> A human being has an especially close connection to that divine being-ness, which, at times, could be perceived in Diana. ***
> {*in the Ephesian Mysteries*}.
>
> (The original hand-written German text of these lines is in Illustration 4.)

There is no need to consider the initial lines about the influences divine beings present of within the head or limbs of human beings. It is in the later lines that references to the Ephesian Mysteries occur. We need to explore the phrase: "A human being has an especially close connection.." This text was published by persons who interpreted this phrase to refer to Dr.

36

I. Wegman alone, as a specific individual. But this interpretation seems unlikely, because the German phrase here is "ein Menschenwesen" which is ambiguous. It can mean, 'one (specific) human being'. But here it means, "a human being"; that is, any human being. (Part Two has more information about this point.)

The sentence is not about one specific, identifiable, individual, nor about one particular god, but about human nature as such, and how it is inherently linked to divine reality – that is, to the nature of the gods as such.

So, in this part of the notebook, Rudolf Steiner is noting for himself, that in the rituals at Ephesus, the acolytes could experience something deeply inspiring: in the Moon-sphere exist divine qualities which arise in the higher qualities of the human soul, once the spiritual-soul (intuitive spiritual awareness) starts to develop into the actual Spiritual-self. We shall see that the spiritual-soul is identified by Rudolf Steiner as 'Mysa'.

The 'spiritual-soul' means the capacity, or strand of consciousness, in us which is capable of intuitive insights, as distinct from intellectual, logical thinking. The 'Spiritual-self' is higher; it is the first of three actual eternal spiritual parts of our being. It arises as the intuitive consciousness is enhanced and also the emotional and intellectual capacities are refined and ennobled.

Note: now a kind of personal, formal vow follows in this notebook entry; presumably this vow was made in antiquity by many acolytes at Ephesos, over the centuries. And it is here that the acrostic occurs. The first word of each line in German, together spell 'Artemüsia'.

"When you, protector-ess of my name,

taught me, giving me inner direction,
I entered the pathways of Gods:
earnestly uniting to *that* soul {*who is*}
central to the spiritual fraternity
{*of Ephesos*},
over whose earthly striving –
since remote human ages –
I, as soul-being of a friend,
am (*i.e., was pre-destined*) to be radiating
liberating 'light-breath'."

The German text of the vow
Als du, meines Namens Schützerin,
richtung weisend mich belehrtest
trat ich ein in Götterbahnen;
ernst mich einend jener Seele
mitten in den Geistverein,
über deren Erdenstreben
seit den grauen Menschenzeiten
ich als Freundes-Seelenwesen
atemlicht befreiend strahlen soll.

Lets examine this remarkable text.

Notes on two phrases in this text
"protector-ess of my name": this phrase refers to
Diana-Artemis, who was also known in some ancient
texts as "Mysia", and this name suggests that she was
helping the more advanced 'Mysa' acolytes. That is,
acolytes who had achieved something of the spiritual-
soul, and thus could be nurtured by the goddess
during the initiatory rituals in the festival.

"which could at times be perceived in Diana"
This tells us that **some** of the acolytes had enough
clairvoyance to perceive, **at times**, the higher energies
within Diana, whilst others did not.

The last section of these notes, which starts with,
"When you, protector-ess of my name", is a kind of
vow or *Summary of Spiritual Purpose*, relevant to all
of the acolytes there. The odd word 'Artemüsia' does
not appear to exist in the ancient Greek language: but

it is a combination of 'Artemis' and 'Musia': this latter word is an alternative name of Demeter.[32] So the acrostic is referring to the Artemis and Demeter initiation path. We noted above, the Artemis-Diana experience led the acolyte on to the higher goddess Demeter, who is an aspect of the divine world.

From these brief notebook entries we can see that their esoteric comments are defined as containing a part of what was actually taught in spiritual realms by the great Archangel Michael. The entry in the notebook also reveals that during the 15th to 18th centuries the great Archangel was instructing souls who were not as yet incarnate.

This is a very potent revelation, and one which is explained in his 1924 lecture cycle, "Karmic Relationships". In brief, Rudolf Steiner reveals in 1924 that many souls were shown core aspects of esoteric wisdom, both the new Mysteries of the 20th century, inaugurated by Rudolf Steiner, as well as the ancient Mysteries such as those of Ephesos.

The next point in these notes is that a Moon-being called 'Isrenum' brought about this change. Again we cannot spend time on this, as there is no other information available about this spirit-being to help us. But we can note that this being is Moon-associated, and consequently is close to Diana.

So the acolyte, after being initiated in the Mysteries of Artemis, (which is about the Word or the Logos, and the spiritual forces in the Macrocosm), progressed on, to enter the Demeter Mysteries. So Isrenum is also associated with Demeter. But we now need to focus again on these words in the notebook:

A (*any*) human being has an

---

[32] The ancient writer Pausanius records that the ancient Argive leader, Mysios/Musios, built the temple at Pellene, from which Demeter received the alternative name of Musias/Mysias.

especially close connection to
that divine being-ness
which, at times,
could be perceived in Diana.

These words are indicating that the initiated acolytes at Ephesos could experience as 'Artemis', the macrocosmic forces of the planets and the zodiac, **from which our own soul derives**. Precisely this same point is taught by Rudolf Steiner in the second of his 1924 'First Class' Lessons,

> ...perceiving within a retrospective view of oneself, becomes the first stage of self-knowledge; (*this brings about*) self-knowledge which is still preparatory for the actual entry into the true, genuine, self-knowledge. For entry into that true self-knowledge unveils to us spiritual, cosmic cognizing **of that Being who is one with our own human being-ness**.[33]
>
> (emphasis mine, AA)

Diana-Artemis was firstly, as we noted above, "The entire spiritual activity within the world's ethers, within the cosmic ethers". But then, on a deeper level, we also learnt that,

> "Those who were able to let the arrangements of this place of consecration exert its influence upon them, this person actually became fully located within this forming process, which was occurring in the sunlight; the sunlight which the Moon was transforming. Then there resounded to that acolyte, as if resounding forth to them from the Sun, I O A."

So now, we can again consider the enigmatic phrase above, "soul-being of a friend",

> I, as soul-being of a friend,
> am to be radiating liberating 'light-breath'.

---

[33]*Esoterische Unterweisung für die Freien Hochschule for Geisteswissenschft am Goetheanum*, Book 1, p 47.

It appears that this phrase is indicating that any of these acolytes at Ephesus who did make some progress towards the 'cosmic human' stage, would be in effect, a 'soul-friend' of "*that* soul {*who is*} central to the spiritual fraternity {*of Ephesos*}".

We can conclude that this special 'central soul' is the spiritual archetype of the human soul, the IOA-bearer, existing in the Moon-sphere. That means, this soul is the same entity as "that beingness-of-the-Gods which at times, could be perceived in Diana". So this special being is what we can understand as our Spiritual-self or cosmic-self, but experienced as having the cosmic IOA forces resonating through it.

This in turn means that the central focus of the Ephesian Mysteries was a spiritual being in the Moon sphere. That is, a being who is a cosmic aspect or cosmic matrix of our own higher soul qualities, (not a particular incarnate human person).

This initiatory quest of the Ephesian acolyte suggests that this 'cosmic soul' itself, which the acolytes at Ephesos could at times experience, was itself seeking to bring about an enhancing of earthly consciousness within these acolytes. This deity was doing this in such a way that the acolyte's soul could manifest this cosmic soul (which is in effect, the Spiritual-self), that is, could become a vessel of it.

Such a student of the Ephesian Mysteries had the task of striving to allow his or her spiritual forces to bring into existence ever more this higher soul-quality, or 'cosmic' soul. We can see from this notebook entry that such a transformation of the earthly ego-sense in spiritual seekers, down here on the Earth, was the primary aim of the 'cosmic soul'.

Finally, we need to explore the two lines in the centre of the latter part of the verse. These lines are saying that the acolytes themselves have had a special initiatory striving pre-arranged for their karma, deriving from earlier times. That is, a karma to be radiating out help to a special soul, once they have joined the Artemis cult, in a later lifetime. That special soul is the 'cosmic self' in the moon sphere, which was a central focus of the Artemis cult:

> earnestly uniting to *that* soul
> central in the spiritual fraternity {*of Ephesos*},
> over whose earthly striving
> since remote human ages
> I, as soul-being of a friend,
> am to be radiating liberating 'light-breath'.

These lines are about a lofty task of initiates and acolytes: namely to help this special being – an aspect of one's own Spirit-self – with its intentions to provide the impetus to encourage an acolyte to awaken to this cosmic, higher self. A similar aim would have been present for acolytes in the Mysteries of other deities.

This text also tells us, that this mission on the Earth was karmically ordained for these acolytes, ever since 'remote human Ages'. The Ephesian Mysteries probably began about 900 BC, so if these acolytes had this task pre-allotted to them karmically, as a future prospect, then this mission must have been set in motion some millennia before the Ephesian lifetime. The verse is declaring that the acolyte **is to now start being of help** (by "radiating liberating light-breath"); that is, as they entered the Ephesian Mysteries, in the centuries before the time of Christ.

Chapter Four: Hierao, Mysa, the Spirit-self and Artemis

Another notebook entry has several unusual terms, including the word 'Hierao'.[34] This word does not exist in Greek. However, a part of it is a Greek word, which means 'to be a priest or a priestess'. Whereas a similar word, 'hieros' is a real word and means 'holy'. This is very relevant here, for at Ephesos the priests and priestesses were called "hierioi" meaning, 'holy ones'. So in the first place we can feel the specially coined word 'Hierao' is in effect, evoking the image of a human being moving towards the holiness which is associated with becoming a priest or priestess.

That would have been a general goal for the acolytes in the Mysteries. Fortunately, we can contemplate the meaning of this odd word 'Hierao' in depth, because in late 1923, Rudolf Steiner jotted down for himself two meditative sketches about this word 'Hierao'. We shall explore these two sketches after first contemplating the note-book entry:

This private notebook entry also has the name 'Mysa' in it, and following on from what we now know of 'Mysa', this name in the notebook entry applies to the acolytes at Ephesos. It refers to their self or ego-sense, as it strives towards the Spiritual-self, under the guidance of the Mysteries of Artemis. So in this verse, 'Mysa' refers to any acolyte at Ephesos who was succeeding in developing the 'Mysa' quality, or spiritual-intuitive consciousness.

Note that words enclosed in these red coloured square brackets, [   ] are added by me. This is to distinguish them from all the other words placed in this kind of bracket ( ); these are from Rudolf Steiner. As he wrote out the text, he placed some words in

---

[34] Published in *The Mission of Rudolf Steiner & Ita Wegman*, Kirchner-Bockholt, p. 59, German edition (Ref.5)

brackets. So all the brackets in the following text are specifically put there by Rudolf Steiner, except those few in red square brackets which are from this author. To prevent the verse being separated into two pages, this verse is presented in full, over the page.[35]

---

[35] In *Rudolf Steiner's Mission*, by Kirchner-Bockholt, (Ref.5).

Notebook entry by Rudolf Steiner

"Mysa, within thy being, seek in thy self:
radiant in [a] radiant world –
[your] being manifests,
and the cosmic Primal Thought-Guides (Kyriotaetes)
they feel themselves as cosmic radiance, beholding,
In human radiance,
In such feeling there came into being:
Hierao (from Mysa)

And the cosmic Primal Forces-of-Being (Dynameis)
they, beholding, directed the cosmic radiance
into human radiance,
in such directing there came into being:
Hierao (from Mysa)

And the cosmic Primal Forming-Powers (Exusiai)
they, beholding, form the cosmic radiance
into human radiance,
in such forming there came into being:
Hierao (from Mysa)."

The [above] words [are what], Hierao's being says
to my soul, from firmly determined, very old karma.

And faltering brings faltering of worlds.
Demons must fail:
good beings of
the Primal-Powers (Archai) * and
cosmic Directing-Powers (Archangels) and
Powers who guide human beings (Angels)
must triumph.

The German text:

Mysa, in deinem Wesen such in dich
Strahlend in strahlender Welt
Offenbart das Wesen sich
Und der Welten-Ur-Gedankenführer (Kyriotetes)
Sie fühlen sich schauend
Als Weltenstrahlen
In Menschenstrahlen
In solchem Fühlen
Ward: Hierao (aus Mysa)
Und der Welten-Ur-Wesenskräfte (Dynamis)
Sie lenkten schauend
Die Weltenstrahlen
In solchem Lenken
Ward: Hierao (aus Mysa)
Und der Welten-Ur-Gestaltungskräfte (Exusiai)
Sie bilden schauend
Die Weltenstrahlen
In solchem Bilden
Ward: Hierao (aus Mysa)
Das sagt Hierao's Wesen
Meiner Seele aus uralten
Festgefügtem Karma:
Und Wanken bringt
Wanken von Welten.
Dämonen müssen verlieren;
Guter Wesen Urkräfte (Angeloi)   [=Archai]*
Und Weltenlenkemächte (Archangeloi)
Und Menschen Führerschaften (Angeloi)
müssen siegen

* This line erroneously has 'Angels' here instead of 'Archai'.[36] We need to remind ourselves that the entire verse was written from his sick-bed. In this text, we have a wonderful portrayal of how the personified

---

[36] The translation 'archetypal forces of good Beings' is not helpful, as 'Urkräfte' is an alternative title for the Archai, and cannot be split.

higher spirituality, 'Hierao', through which one becomes a priest of the Mysteries, arises from the 'Mysa' or the spiritual-soul – and the assistance given by divine-spiritual beings to this effort. The spiritual energies in these divine beings in the Moon-sphere **are the cosmic matrix of the spiritual-soul or Mysa.**

So in this verse, the acolyte is urged to cognize how her or his higher ego-sense (Mysa) is permeated by, and sustained by, hierarchical beings, and how this awareness brings into being within the acolyte what we call today the 'Spiritual-self'.

So, through the blessings of various higher divine-spiritual beings, there arises out of the personal 'Mysa', the spiritual qualities of the Spiritual-self. Thus did the sanctified quality of a priest or priestess (Hierao) come into being in the Ephesian Mysteries.

In the last part of the verse, the acolyte receives an admonition from the higher awareness of the 'Hierao-quality'. This inspired the acolyte to try to bring about a spiritual renewal of humanity, to ensure a positive future. We shall explore this notebook entry in more detail later, after exploring the other indications about the Artemis Mysteries. We now need to contemplate the 'Hierao' word more closely. The above notebook entry becomes more meaningful as we explore the two meditative texts and diagrams about this word, mentioned above.[37]

But before we encounter these, it would be helpful if the relationships between the various deities that have been mentioned, are made clear. We have mentioned Artemis-Diana, Demeter, Persephone or Proserpina, Mysa, Iackhos and Dionysos. The following page shows the relationship of these deities to each other. Part Two provides more detailed information about them, from various sources.

---

[37] From GA 268, p.94-95

The Greek deities and the human being

Dionysos: the earthly ego-sense
when this is impelled towards morality it produces,

Mysa and Iackhos: these represent the spiritual-soul with elements of the Spiritual-self

Artemis-Diana assists Mysa and Iackhos to become more spiritualized, and to attain perception of the ether realm, in the Moon sphere.

An acolyte can advance beyond the Artemis process to that of: **Demeter** (or 'Musia')
Demeter represents the deity from whom human consciousness has arisen, but this consciousness must be so understood that it can arise from spiritual forces **active in the vicinity of the Earth**…thus Demeter is the primal being of the Earth.[38] Demeter is also the divine creator of the eternal spirit in the human being… the same divine tapestry of energies which created the Earth.[39]

The 'daughter' of Demeter is **Persephone** (or **Proserpina**: this means that the influence on the acolyte of experiencing the divine matrix of the Earth's aura (Demeter), leads to a clairvoyant consciousness developing. This state is called Persephone or Proserpina.

Kore (or Core) is the same as Persephone or Proserpina. But ancient myths report that Mysa is the same 'deity' or human spiritual quality, as Kore. So the outcome for the acolyte of undergoing the Demeter Mysteries is similar, in some ways, to that of the Artemis Mysteries.

That Kore represents basically the same spiritual reality as Mysa (and Iackhos) is confirmed by Rudolf

---

[38] In GA 8 p.95
[39] ibid.

Steiner's words about the Ephesian Mysteries, which we noted earlier, "...behind these nature elements, the pupil was conscious of Persephone, the daughter of Demeter (*or Ceres*), actively present as the non-material foundation of all substance; to this 'Goddess' all the elements are obedient."

FIRST 'HIERAO' NOTE FROM RUDOLF STEINER: [40]

I take you into that Spirit-circle which may regard itself as summoned forth by the Spirits of the Sun, and which is permitted to declare that, the Lunar Spirits transform this impulse, within Cosmic Wisdom.

Have you the Will to hear my Word from out of this Spirit?

```
2  16  12  6  4
o   o   o   o  o
H   I   E   R  A  O
```

If you feel yourself in this Spirit-word, then
the Spirits of the Solar and Lunar Encirclings
shall perceive and acknowledge you.

They shall enable you to encounter them;
or else if you allow this Spirit-word to fall away
from your heart, they would have to push you
away from them.

Imagine yourself seated on a branch of a tree –
it supports you, for your Word is radiant
in spirit-heights –
but if you speak-forth something not justified,
then you cut away the branch,
from underneath yourself
and you fall into the Abyss.

Note: The being who is speaking, the "I" in the first line, appears to be the Hierao.

---

[40] In GA 268, p. 94-95.

SECOND 'HIERAO' NOTE: TEXT AND GRAPHIC

Seek the Seven everywhere, wherever something is of a spiritual nature, or where something happens of a spiritual nature.
Cognize, that what is in the Cosmos, is also in you, and what is in you, is also in the Cosmos.

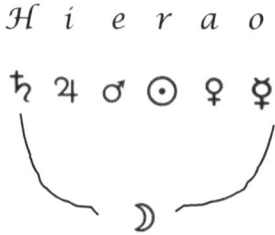

$$\mathcal{H} \quad i \quad e \quad r \quad a \quad o$$

$$\hbar \quad 4 \quad \sigma \quad \odot \quad ♀ \quad ☿$$

$$☽$$

THIRD HIERAO TEXT AND GRAPHIC

Behold: each of these (seven planets) disappear in a spiral, and return into being again.

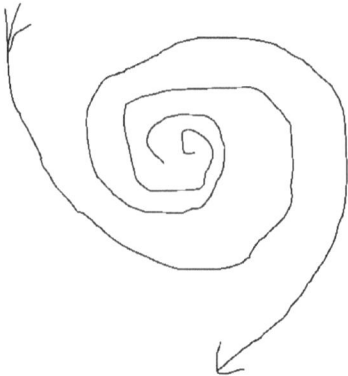

Commentary:

From the first two of these sketches, it becomes clear that 'hierao' is a term for high astral qualities from the 7 classical 'planets' of astrology. Each of these planets has a letter assigned to it. But the most important thing about the Hierao is, that it is a kind of 'cosmic' that is, planetary, version of the human being: it consists of the planetary sounds which resonate in us. As the sketch says: "*..what is in the Cosmos, is also in you...*"

It is also significant that Rudolf Steiner drew the two curved lines which envelop the moon. These indicate that these planetary ('cosmic') astral forces have been received into the Moon-sphere. This tells us that the mysterious 'cosmic self' which was the core deity of the Artemis Mysteries, is this same 'Hierao', which Artemis nurtured.

Artemis-Diana nurtured this cosmic matrix of the human Higher-self, and made it ready for the acolytes, within the Moon-sphere, for Artemis is a Moon goddess. So therefore this 'cosmic self', this Hierao, is very likely "that soul, central in the spiritual fraternity {*of Ephesos*}".

Hierao includes the IAO, which as we saw earlier, is used as the name of the Divine, and the divine potential in the human being: these three sounds represent the highest spiritual qualities of Mercury, Venus and Jupiter. In the Hierao one understands that the finest qualities of the planets involved are present – and become present in the acolyte once he or she reaches the 'Mysa' stage.

Therefore the above meditative notebook entry (p.44) says "…..**there came into being: Hierao (from Mysa)**".

That the finest qualities of the planets are meant, is indicated by the numbers in the sketch, for they are referring to the chakras, which are the especial centres in the aura which cause clairvoyance.

```
2  16  12   6  4
o   o   o   o  o
H   I   E   R  A   O
```

  2: the forehead chakra
16: the throat chakra
12: the heart chakra
6 & 4: two chakras lower down in the body

With the 'Hierao', we have a similar but more comprehensive cosmic (planetary) signifier of the human being, than the IAO. These letters are vowels which are associated with specific planets. But there are some differences from the accepted vowel-planet values as given by Rudolf Steiner in his lectures on Eurythmy. Saturn here has the 'h' sound, instead of the 'u' sound, and the Sun here has 'r', a vocalic, mobile consonant, instead of 'au'.

Also the 'i' and the 'o' are transposed; in reality 'o' belongs to Jupiter and 'i' to Mercury. Then, below all this in the sketch, is the Moon, signifying that these planetary qualities are held in the Moon sphere - the sphere of Artemis.

The reason for these different vowel/consonant allocations is unknown, but it is likely that the ancient Greeks wanted a 'word' which both referred to the planetary forces and also resembled their word for 'sacred' and for 'priest/priestess', which is, as saw earlier, 'hierioi'.

We can also conclude that when those acolytes, fortunate enough to be initiated successfully at Ephesos, brought forth this cosmic-self aspect from the Mysa or Iackhos quality (the spiritual-soul), it could then be said of such an acolyte, that they had experienced the truth of the following words....

    A human being has an especially close
    connection to that

divine being-ness,
which was perceived in Diana.

Diana or Artemis holds the matrix of those 'Hierao' planetary influences which leads to the emergence of the Spiritual-self in the acolyte.

The third notebook entry, about the planets disappearing into a spiral and then re-emerging, is not revealing more about the planetary qualities, but rather is an exercise for oneself to help the meditant to become more inwardly connected to these energies.

We can now explore the verse from Rudolf Steiner given to Ita Wegman on her birthday in 1925. This text has the words 'Mysa' and 'Artemisia' in it.

Again, to avoid the verse being separated over two pages, it is placed on the next page in full:

A birthday verse for Dr. I. Wegman
(22nd Feb. 1925)[41]

Shining over the world-enigma is
the spirit out-raying light of Ephesus,
from out of cosmic-depths –
where exists the Divine-spiritual.
It shines.

There descends upon the image
of the Goddess
the soul-supporting light of Ephesus,
in the soul-depths of the Goddess –
where exists human being-ness.
It descends.

In the light of Ephesus' mystae site
my heart rayed forth, long ago,
Mysa's being-ness – mirror image
of Artemüsia, so actively present.
It rayed out warmly.

The gaze of the friend
turned backwards in the course of time
finds the delicate being of Mysa
moving around the image of the goddess.
Delicately contemplative.

This verse arose from Rudolf Steiner's contemplation of the activity undertaken at Ephesos, long ago. In referring to "Mysa" it is referring to the result of the inner work undertaken by all the acolytes there, rather than specifically referring solely to Dr. Wegman. However, it is also directly relevant to her as a meditative exercise, since it is understood that in a past life, she had been an acolyte there.

The German text follows on the following page.

---

[41] In *Rudolf Steiner's Mission*, by Kirchner-Bockholt, (Ref.5).

For the 22nd. Februar 1925

Es leuchtet über der Rätselwelt
Ephesus' geiststrahlendes Licht
Aus den Weltentiefen
Wo Göttlich-Geistiges waltet
  Leuchtet es.

Es fallet über der Göttin Bild
Ephesus' seelentragendes Licht
In der Göttin Seelentiefe
Wo Menschen-Wesen waltet
  Fallet es.

Im Lichte von Ephesus Mystenstatt
Da strahlte dereinst mein Herz
Mysa's Wesen Abbild
Der waltenden Artemisia   [Artemüsia ?]
  Es strahlte warm.

Des Freundes Schauen
Rückgewandt im Zeitenlauf
Findet Mysa's zartes Wesen
Webend um der Götter Bild
  Zart sinnend.

The first line of the second quatrain, "*There descends upon the image of the Goddess...*" is complex; it could also be translated as, "*Making luminous the image of the Goddess*". In any event, it speaks of the radiance which the acolyte in their meditation feels is enveloping the statue.[42] The third line tells us that this light is living within the core of the goddess.

---

[42] Literally translated, this line is, "There *descends upon* the image of the Goddess, the soul-bearing light". But the German verb here, 'fallen', with its preposition 'über', has much more sophisticated nuances, including that of implying an imbuing action, which makes the statue subtly glow: "Making luminous the image of the Goddess is the light.." This alternative removes the directional aspect (of the light 'falling' or 'descending'); which is unlikely to be

We need to explore this third line, "*the soul-depths of the Goddess – where exists human being-ness*". The picture presented here is very striking, and has a deep esoteric meaning. In identifying a divine being as the matrix of the human being, we are learning that the Spiritual-self of a human being can be thought of, in some way, as deriving from the 'substance' of the influences raying in from the combined deities, Artemis-Müsia (i.e., Artemis-Demeter) radiance. It is precisely this truth which we have just been discovering; and which another notebook entry also confirms, as we shall soon see.

The third verse, "*...my heart rayed forth, long ago Mysa's being*" is revealing that acolytes at Ephesos underwent the challenge of trying to have the high spiritual energies of their own spiritual-soul so empowered, and so livingly, actively present, that the spiritual-soul could emerge. And emerge in such a way that through the assistance of Artemis, their Spiritual-self or 'Hierao' could arise.

As we noted earlier, the spiritual-soul means the capacity, or strand of consciousness, in us which is capable of intuitive insights, which is quite different from intellectual, logical thinking. The Spiritual-self arises as the intuitive consciousness is enhanced and also the emotional and intellectual capacities are refined and ennobled.

So, we learn from these verses that the acolyte's soul and spirit became what the priests there referred to as 'Mysa', which is a personification of spiritual forces invoked from the astral realm. This 'Mysa-nature' has the possibility to resonate with influences from Artemis. This inner development was undertaken in the magnificent temple of Artemis, and was a core part of the secret esoteric rituals undertaken there. As we shall see, this obviously had

---

meant, as the light is said to be within the being of the Goddess.

nothing to do with any popular festival which was later somewhat flippantly named 'the Artemisia' by Romans.

This stage of becoming an 'hierao' was the beginning of the initiatory experience. We can know this because, as the above lecture extracts reveal, the acolytes were also seeking to arise consciously into the Moon sphere, and experience the cosmic nature of the human being. So this activity would bring to birth the cosmic Self (which we can understand as the Spiritual-self).

Or at least it would help the advanced acolytes to spiritually experience this cosmic Self in the Moon-sphere. It was especially through the help of Artemis or Artemis-Müsia (Demeter) that this meditative effort was made, so that the influences from the Moon-sphere could then help the acolyte move towards their high goal of achieving their Spiritual-self.

The term, 'mystae site', also in the third verse, is an ancient Greek term, and means a site where the Mysteries were undertaken. Rudolf Steiner uses this word often in his Mystery Plays, where it is often mistranslated as 'mystic'.

The last quatrain, "...*finds the delicate being of Mysa moving around the image of the goddess*" is pointing out the gentle, feminine qualities that the spiritual-soul nature manifests. This would be consistent with what Rudolf Steiner described as a central challenge of the Ephesian Mysteries: the demand that the acolytes became selfless and humble, and not self-centred, assertive people.[43]

Now, in the light of all that we have been learning about Mysa, Hierao, and the Ephesian initiation

---

[43] In GA 126, Occult History, lect. 30th Dec. 1910.

experience, we can return to the profound central verse we explored earlier.

The private notebook entry about the Hierarchies and 'Hierao'

"Mysa, within thy being, seek in thy self:
radiant in [a] radiant world –
[your] being manifests,
and the cosmic Primal Thought-Guides (Kyriotaetes)
they feel themselves as cosmic radiance, beholding,
in human radiance,
In such feeling there came into being:
Hierao (from Mysa)

And the cosmic Primal Forces-of-Being (Dynameis)
they, beholding, directed the cosmic radiance
into human radiance,
in such directing there came into being:
Hierao (from Mysa)

And the cosmic Primal Forming-Powers (Exusiai)
they, beholding, form the cosmic radiance
into human radiance,
In such forming there came into being:
Hierao (from Mysa)."

The [above] words [are what], Hierao's being says
to my soul, from firmly determined, very old karma.

And faltering brings faltering of worlds.
Demons must fail;
good beings of
the Primal-Powers (*Archai*) * and
cosmic Directing-Powers (*Archangels*) and
Powers who guide human beings (*Angels*)
must triumph.

This text brings together all of the points mentioned or implied in the other writings from Rudolf Steiner about Ephesos.

Verse One tells us that if an acolyte can develop the spiritual-soul (that is, an intuitive, spiritually-perceptive consciousness), then, helped by the presence of Artemis, the noble radiance of the spiritual-soul (i.e., Mysa) as it rays forth, is received by the Kyriotaetes – the Spirits of Wisdom in the Jupiter sphere – and they feel as if they are gazing out, from within this radiance. This interaction of the spiritual-soul with these hierarchical deities brings forth the Spiritual-self. This Spiritual-self is viewed here as a microcosm of the planetary spheres, and called 'the Hierao'.

Verse Two tells us that the Dynameis or Spirits of Movement in the Mars sphere, more specifically guide this highly spiritual, or devachanic, radiance into the acolyte's germinal Spiritual-self, that is, into her or his devachanic aura. Thereby bringing the Spiritual-self, (the Hierao) more strongly into reality.

Then, Verse Three reveals that the sun-gods, the Powers or Exusiai from the sun-sphere, mould this radiance, so that it is ever more a radiance which becomes part of the human being; of his or her Spiritual-self, the Hierao.

The next sentence tells us that once the majestic macrocosmic aspect of the Spiritual-self is present, it then informs the acolyte of two facts. Firstly that, on the basis of such achievement by the acolyte – achieved with the inner help of the gods – the beings of the Third Hierarchy – Principalities (Archai), Archangels and Angels – are enabled to oppose ahrimanic powers.

Secondly we learn that this initiatory struggle at Ephesos was karmically ordained, long ago. So some millennia before the lifetime at Ephesos, this karmic mission was established as a positive future opportunity. The cause of the karmic mission, established several millennia ago, would appear to have its origin in even earlier lifetimes.

The last section of the text is a positive expression of hope that the Third Hierarchy (the Principalities, Archangels and Angels) can assist the above process, thus conquering the demonic powers who seek to destroy humanity.

The Hierao is then, those highest spiritual forces from the solar system which are relevant to human beings; in effect, the Hierao is the Spiritual-self becoming actively present in the human being.

I have attempted to unveil and clarify the meaning of brief words from Rudolf Steiner about the awe-inspiring processes that prevailed in the Mysteries of Artemis, at Ephesos, the site of "distinguished academies".

The light raying forth from Ephesos could live on in the souls of those who were acolytes there, and still today encourage a feeling for the spiritual reality of life, including the cosmic forces active in speech. This could also include what we refer to as astrology, and also a keen sensitivity to the 'living Earth'. That is, its ecological wonders and the influence on our soul of the seasonal cycle of the year, especially those active from within the etheric aura of the Earth.

****

PART TWO Appendices

APPENDIX ONE
Mysa, Demeter, Iackhos, Dionysos

Misa / Mysa / Kore

Both Rudolf Steiner's notebook entries and his verses refer to a certain "Mysa". So, what does the name refer to? Academically, it is known that Mysa is a spiritual being, only briefly referred to in ancient Greek texts, who was revered in the secretive Mysteries of Orpheus and Dionysos. Both of these cults are closely linked to the cult of Artemis.

There are one or two texts from Rudolf Steiner where he uses 'Mysa' as a generic name for the Spiritual-self, not referring specifically to any of the acolytes in a Mystery Centre.[44] So what is this name about? We need to bear in mind that Greek gods and goddesses can be personifications of spiritual realities.

Misa (in Greek, Μισα) is also called Mysa (in Greek, Μυσα); this name is also spelt Mise (Μιση) or Mises (Μισης). This goddess, under any of these names, is identified as being close to, or the daughter of, Dionysos. She also has a masculine aspect, a twin brother, called Iackhos, (see below for more about this deity).

Furthermore, one inscription, from the Aeolic town of Kyme, identifies the deity Core or Kore with Mysa (Mise/Mises/Misa), whom we shall from now on refer to as 'Mysa'.[45] On this basis then, Mysa is also Persephone, since as we noted earlier, Kore and Persephone are identical. This means that Mysa is

---

[44] Dr. Wegman received a birthday-verse entitled "to Mysa" in 1924. This title appears to indicate that the verse is dedicated to the quest for Mysa, or the spiritual-soul, as undertaken at Ephesos.

[45] Inscription DXCV, in the British Museum.

related to Demeter, the Earth goddess, for Demeter is the mother of Kore or Persephone (or Mysa).

Since Mysa is placed by Rudolf Steiner as a central spiritual being (or personification) in the Mysteries of Artemis, it is natural that in the above extracts of his teachings about Ephesos, both Demeter and Persephone are mentioned. It is known to scholars that, in antiquity, once a year a festival was held at Ephesos dedicated to Demeter. When this custom commenced and for how long it continued is unknown.[46]

Mysa and Demeter

An ancient text about Mysa, one of the Orphic hymns (no. 42), refers to her as the "Earth-mother". But this appears to be an inaccurate definition, because she was really Persephone, the daughter of the Earth-mother, Demeter. We have seen from Rudolf Steiner, that the term 'Earth-mother' refers to the spiritual forces from the cosmos which sustain the fertile Earth. So the 'daughter' of the Earth-Mother is in effect the human soul; but from Rudolf Steiner's texts we can see that Mysa means the soul on its way to spirituality. That is developing the spiritual-soul, and moving towards the Spiritual-self.

So the reference to Mysa in the Orphic hymn indicates that there is a close connection between Demeter and Mysa. But also, Demeter herself is sometimes called by a somewhat similar name: Mysia/Musia after the name of a temple, dedicated to her in Achaea, called the Musaeon.[47]

---

[46] This custom is attested in a letter from AD 84, addressed to a Roman official, the proconsul of 'Asia', Mestius Florus.
[47] The temple is named after the Argive hero, Musias/Mysius, who had the temple built near Pellene. There was another temple to her near Argos. Herodotus mentions a temple to Demeter in Achaea where "secret rites were performed".
[48] GA 232, *Mystery Centres*, lect. 14.Dec. 23

These names, Musia or Mysia, being similar to 'Mysa', indicate a close association between Demeter, the 'Earth-Mother' – the primary astral energies of our planet's aura – and the qualities which Mysa represents. For as we noted earlier, and shall explore in more detail below, Mysa represents the spiritual potential of the human being.

Mysa as Kore
Now, noting that Mysa is also Kore, we can start to understand more deeply the meaning of this word. Rudolf Steiner's private notes clarify the situation further. For Kore is an ancient Greek word usually meaning 'virgin' or 'young woman'. But it was also used in the famous phrase, "The Virgin of the World" (or the Cosmos Virgin).

But here one realizes that a change needs to be made to the expression "The Virgin of the World". This phrase is not about a specific goddess, but about the vibrant, pure spirituality permeating the cosmos: the *Divine Soul of the World*. The Greek term Kore here **does not mean a young woman**; in this phrase, Kore means 'spiritual being-ness of high purity'. This is also a fine definition of Mysa or the spiritual-soul quality. Mysa is then a personification of spirituality. In fact, Kore was also used in a similar way for the human eyes, as the expression of the soul shining through our eyes.

Dionysos
Rudolf Steiner reveals that the deity called Dionysos represents the emerging ego-sense in humanity; and this ego-sense can of course, be spiritualized, moving towards the Spiritual-self via the spiritual-soul (that is, from the development of intuitive sense-free consciousness). From Rudolf Steiner's brief remarks and also from some mythological information, we can conclude that Mysa and Iackhos are terms for the spiritual-soul arising up to the Spiritual-self; in a feminine and in a masculine sense, but in the context of the initiation process offered in the Mysteries.

We learn from an ancient inscription, that Dionysos was experienced as being associated with Demeter – the force that confers higher consciousness on the initiated acolyte. Plutarch notes in his *Antiquities*, (section 27) that a festival in honour of Dionysos was celebrated yearly at Ephesos.

Iackhos
As we noted above, Iackhos is called the son of Dionysos, and it is very significant that a statue of Iackhos was placed in Athens, in a temple dedicated to Demeter, located near the entrance to the procession pathway which led to the initiation centre of Eleusis. Iackhos was holding a burning lantern, a clear indicator that the pathway to initiation was via the higher consciousness of the Spiritual-self. Rudolf Steiner indicated Iackhos was pointing to the 'Christ-child', which can be understood as the Spiritual-self.[48]

There is another important aspect to Iackhos, known from the Mysteries. One epithet used for Artemis in ancient Greek literature, is '*Iackunthotorophos*' (Ἰακυνθοτοροφος); which means 'nurturer of Iackhos'. So 'Iackhos' refers to a spiritual potential in the human being, a potential which the influence of Artemis nurtures into full blossoming.[49] Since Iackhos and Mysa are two aspects of the same spiritual reality, it is not surprising that Demeter is also the nurturer of Mysa.

Mysa and Iackhos in summary
Putting all of this into an anthroposophical context, it appears that Mysa and Iackhos represent the spiritual qualities in the soul higher than the normal earthly ego-sense (which Dionysos represents). So they are a personification of a higher soul quality, a quality which is emerging from the spiritualizing ego-sense. We recall here that, at times, the Greek gods and goddesses are personifications of spiritual realities.

---

[49] E. Schwyzer (*Griechische Grammatik*), 1939, noted in Liddell & Scott *Greek-English Dictionary*, p.814b.

So, in regard to the human being, especially the acolyte in the Mysteries, Mysa and Iackhos represent the spiritual-soul, or the intuitive thinking capacity, as it strives towards the Spiritual-self.

The spiritual-soul manifests as the capacity for spiritual thinking develops; and this culminates in higher insights, often experienced as intuitive flashes. The Spiritual-self manifests when these higher insights, together with a purified, chaste feeling-life, and a selflessness born of good-will, become a permanent reality for the acolyte; when these become the 'self' of that person.

But as we shall see, Mysa (and Iackhos) is therefore **a vessel of those spiritual forces** which, held by higher beings, **are the cosmic (planetary) matrix from which the spiritual-soul itself derives**. This expresses the core revelation offered by the Ephesian Mysteries, as we have discussed in Part One.

So the many acolytes, both women and men, at Ephesus over the centuries, were all endeavouring to be a 'Mysa' or an 'Iackhos', that is, someone whose spiritual-soul was moving towards the "cosmic human being" which Rudolf Steiner referred to in the above lecture extract, and which we could consider to be in effect, the Spiritual-self.

APPENDIX TWO
The meaning of 'Artemisia'

As we noted earlier, the word 'Artemisia' occurs only twice in Rudolf Steiner's work. Above one of the entries about Ephesos, in a private notebook, he wrote the heading "Artemisia"; and this word also occurs in the text of another entry. It appears nowhere else in his Complete Works. But as we have noted, these instances may be in error, and that the word Artemüsia was actually meant.

It is fascinating that the word Artemisia, as the name of the sacred initiatory 'festival' in which Artemis is understood to be involved, is itself a 'mystery'. For it is extremely rare in texts written by ancient Greek people.

Generally, scholars regard this word as the name of a festival which was in some way dedicated to the goddess Artemis. The viewpoint has arisen that such a sacred religious-esoteric festival dedicated to this goddess was held every year in the month named after her, *Artemisios*.

However, it is a fact that this word Artemisia, as the name of such a festival, is not allowed to appear in huge official and authoritative classic Greek-English or Greek-German dictionaries. The word 'Artemisia' does occur in these huge dictionaries, but not as the name of a festival to do with Artemis. It is the name of several prominent women in ancient Greece, and also the name of a plant (e.g., wormwood).

The only officially recognized word for this festival, in the huge, authoritative Liddell & Scott *Greek-English Dictionary* is a rare and unusual version: the Artamitia (τα᾿Αρταμιτία). The reason that 'Artemisia' is otherwise not permitted an entry in the great Classic Greek-English or Greek-German dictionaries, as the name for a festival involving Artemis, is not stated.

So I have carried out extensive research into the use of this word in antiquity. It appears that scholars, both English and German, can find no instance of this word being used the ancient Greeks to refer to a sacred, ritualistic festival, that invokes Artemis.[50] Yet this word does exist in ancient Greek texts, and does refer to some kind of Artemis festival.

It appears that the only references to it occur in texts or inscriptions written in the late Grecian era, when Greece was under the control of the Roman Empire. These few instances are about a popular festivity, having athletic games and other popular entertainment as its focus, and not an esoteric Mystery event. This fact seems not to have been noticed by researchers, and as a result, studies on the theme of Artemis can incorrectly point to the word 'Artemisia' existing in texts or inscriptions, which in fact do not contain this word.

For a study of the confusion around this word, including academic references to it in ancient inscriptions which are without any basis see Appendix Four.

---

[50] As with Scott & Liddell, so also with the *Wörterbuch der Griecheschen Eigennamen*, 3 Vols, 1884, by H. Pape, p. 322; and *Handwörterbuch der griechischen Sprache*, F. Passow, 1819-823,p. 326; and 1880, *Wörterbuch der Lexikographie*, H. Sengebush, p.361.

APPENDIX THREE
A closer view of some key Steiner texts

From the Notebook   (see page 38)

> ….A (*any*) human being has an
> especially close connection to
> that divine being-ness
> which, at times,
> could be perceived in Diana.

A (any) human being, or one human being ?

The main point here is that the entire focus of this passage is human nature as specifically contrasted to the nature of the gods. This in turn indicates that it is saying, "any human being", not one specific person.

This conclusion is supported not only by the German text having "Menschenwesen" (human being), not simply "Mensch" (person). It is also supported by the situation that in this notebook, human nature is defined as having a special link to 'Götterwesen' ('being-ness of Gods' or 'Divine-being-ness'), and not simply to 'Götter' (gods).

Which could at times be perceived in Diana"
                (see page 38)

This phrase, "*which could at times be perceived in Diana*" is correct here; not "*which was perceived in Diana*". For the German word is würde, (i.e., 'could be perceived') not wûrde ('was perceived'). The German text is in a scribbled or rough hand-writing, so the markings known as 'Umlauts' are not clearly written, and can be misinterpreted as a simple vowel marking. But Illustration 3 has samples of this same letter written by Rudolf Steiner with an Umlaut, showing that here he used an Umlaut, not a simple vowel marking.

When the Umlaut is used, the verb means 'could at times be perceived', or 'might be perceived'.[51] This tells us that **some** of the acolytes had enough clairvoyance to perceive, **at times**, the higher energies within Diana, whilst others did not.

The Periphery of the body (see page 35)
The first lines of this notebook entry, about the periphery of the human being, are enigmatic. They refer to the point from which in the human body, higher powers could exert an influence. When writing this down Rudolf Steiner was noting, on his sick-bed, that after the extrusion of the moon (which occurred mid-way through the Lemurian Age, some 18 million years ago), the Gods could now experience the limbs, no longer only the head, as the periphery of the body.

That is, these deities had the ability now to influence the lower part of the body, not just the higher part (the head). So the gods could now experience how human limbs – the arms and legs – form a real periphery, reaching out into the environs, much more so than the head. The full implication of this dynamic is unknown, and need not be explored.

Radiating liberating light breath   (see page 35)
The kind of help intended is described as "radiating liberating 'light-breath'"; a striking phrase which is not commented on in the notebook entry. It remains an enigma. Another notebook entry helps to further clarify the interaction of the acolyte at Ephesos with the Hierarchies, but does not help with the 'light-breath' enigma.

From the Birthday Verse for Dr. Wegman   (p. 53)
In the third verse, the words, "*of Artemüsia, so actively present*" has been translated as '*of Artemüsia holding sway*', or 'prevailing' or 'governing', because the German word here (walten-den) has various meanings. It is often used by Rudolf Steiner to refer

---

[51] This is known as the 'subjunctive' mood of the verb.

to the active presence, or existence of, a spiritual being or influence. As noted above, the word here is 'Artemisia', but this appears to be an error.

It is possible that this line means that influences from Artemis and Demeter are experienced as 'ruling' or 'holding sway'. But my preferred alternative: "*of Artemüsia, so actively present*", indicates that these influences are experienced as actively existing, specifically present, in the Moon-sphere, to help the acolyte.

This alternative is supported by the use of the same word (walten) in verse two, where it appears to have the meaning of *actively present*:

...in the soul-depths of the Goddess –
where exists [waltet] human being-ness.

It is unlikely that "*human being-ness*" is 'ruling' or 'prevailing' in the soul-depths of the Goddess.

APPENDIX FOUR
Artemisia: the confusion around this word

As noted earlier, this word has a strangely unclear status in Greek dictionaries. Academic texts can refer to this word as existing in ancient inscriptions, when in fact there are none in these. Such inscriptions may however, include a somewhat similar word, such as 'Artemidi', which means 'for Artemis' or 'Artemidos' which means 'of Artemis'. For example, an archaeologist when writing about this festival in the *American Journal of Archaeology* (Vol 76, No.1, Jan. 1972), had to refer to evidence for this word only in ancient inscriptions, since there appear to be almost no ancient Greek written texts containing this word.

To do this, the researcher chose to cite examples of inscriptions held mainly in the British Museum; of these 3 inscriptions, in one example (no. 482), the word Artemisia actually does not occur, (see Illustration 1). The other two examples each do have this word, but one (no. 606) is about an athlete winning a game in the popular athletic 'Artemisia' festivity; the third (no. 615) is about a commercial transaction being made during athletic festive days in the month dedicated to Artemis. They are part of the records made for the Roman authorities regarding such games (from the reign of Emperor Hadrian and also of Vespasian).[52]

Moreover, the primary article about this festival available on the Internet is, "*Artemisia*" by L. Schmitz, (in W. Smith's *Dictionary of Greek and Roman Antiquities*, 1874).[53] This article refers the reader to several occurrences of this word in ancient texts. But it is a striking fact that none of the ancient writings mentioned by Schmitz as having examples of the

---

[52] Greek Inscriptions in the British Museum; //archive.org /details/ GIBM/IV/; pps. 536, 626, 630-32, E. L. Hicks, Clarendon Press, 1874.
[53] www.Penelope.uchicago.edu/Thayer/Roman/Texts...

word 'Artemisia' actually contain this word. For example, the *Pythian Odes* by Pindar (II,12) are given by Schmitz as a reference, but in fact this Pindar text does not mention this word.

A similar reference to the word Artemisia as existing in ancient writings, was made about 1903, in the huge German-language "Wissowa-Pauly Encyclopaedia of Antiquity". In its article "Artemisia', it states that the Greco-Roman writer, Thucydides, mentions this word as meaning the festival for Artemis.[54] The reader is referred to a passage in Thucydides (bk.3,104:5); but in fact a perusal of this Greek text reveals that this passage does not include this word at all, see Illustration 2.

What I have concluded from all of this, is that there appears to be no usage of this word for a sacred, initiatory event, by the Greeks in their 'Golden Age', prior to the Romans becoming their over-lords. There are several examples from the later, fading years of ancient Greek civilisation. One occurrence of 'Artemisia' in a written text, as the name of a festival connected apparently to Artemis, is to be found in a document known as the *Onomastikon* written by Jullis Pollucis, (2nd Cent. AD), he refers to "*Artemis of the Artemisia and of Ephesos*".[55]

But he is referring to the sporting and theatrical festival which was celebrated at Ephesos in March-April, the month of Artemision. Under the rule of the Romans, this was called 'the Artemisia (*festival*)'. One notes that Pollucis, though a Greek scholar, was appointed to his academic position by Roman authorities, and that a prominent Greek literary writer, Lucian of Samosata (125-180 AD) attacked Jullius Pollucis as "an ignorant, debased person".

---

[54] *Artemisia 4*, by Stengel, in the 1903 Pauly-Wissowa Realencyclopädie der Classischen Altertumswissenschaft.
[55] In the Greek of Pollucis "... Ἀρτέμιιδος Ἀρτέμισια καὶ Ἐφέσια, p.37.

A further indicator of the word being used only in an exoteric sense, and only in fading years of the Grecian era, is that a Greek novelist, Xenophon of Ephesos, (1st-2nd centuries AD). Modern writers mention him as referring to the 'Artemisia' festival; but firstly, he wrote about an Artemis 'festival' which was a popular festive time at which both men and women chose their sweethearts. Secondly, he did not even use the word, 'Artemisia', but instead wrote about a time '...of celebrating the *local festival of Artemis*... (Artemidos)'[56]

So it appears that texts produced within the context of the Roman Empire occasionally used the word *Artemisia* for an athletic and theatrical festival, but otherwise the Greeks did not use it for a sacred esoteric festival. Archaeologists report that about 30 inscriptions of the word 'Artemisia' do exist; but most of these are of Roman origin, and almost all refer to prominent women in antiquity, who had that name, or to the non-esoteric popular festival.[57] (It also can be used to refer to multiple temples dedicated to Artemis.)

With regard to Ephesos, there are some 4,000 inscriptions found at Ephesos alone, but it appears that no reference to the Artemisia festival has been found amongst these. So we can again conclude that the ancient Greeks – even at Ephesos itself – did not

---

[56] Xenophon, *Ephesiaca*, Bk.1, Chapt, 2, sect.4: " aegeto taes Artemidos epichoerios heortae " Ἤγετο τῆς Αρτέμιδος ἐπιχώριος ἑορτὴ ...")
[57] I have examined a collection of inscriptions made available for Greek scholars in an electronic database (epigraphy.packhum.org). If a search is made for 'Artemisia' among these inscriptions, some 156 similar words appear. But it appears that the word 'Artemisia' is not there, that is, not as a sacred festival name. Artemisia does occur, but as the name of prominent women named after her, or a plants of this name.

like to use this word.[58] It may have been regarded as flippant and therefore inappropriate for a festival of such a lofty nature. This is itself a powerful indicator as to how strong was the reverence and awe felt by the ancient Greeks of Ephesian Mysteries.

On this point, the modern version of the 'Pauly Encyclopaedia" has deleted the article which stated that 'Artemisia' refers to a festival honouring Artemis. But as with modern classic Greek-English Dictionaries, nothing is said about the usage of the word in the Romanized Greek world for a popular festivity named after Artemis, and specifically called the Artemisia.[59]

In the face of such inconsistencies, we can conclude that people today are generally not aware that the word 'Artemisia' was either not used for this purpose, or very seldom used, by the ancient Greeks. So there is something exceptional about this word; it was culturally taboo because of the reverence in which Artemis was held. But the Romans would have had no reluctance to use it. It is also possible that there was a popular festival centred on Artemis, in the centuries before Roman rule. If so, then the Romans were referring to what had been created as a non-esoteric, popular festival.

Now returning to our contemplation of the initiatory process involving Artemis, in view of the striking lack of references in classical Greek civilisation to a festival for Artemis in general, it appears unlikely that an esoteric Artemis 'festival' was held at Ephesos. So the initiation processes which the

---

[58] John Kampen, *The Cult of Artemis and the Essenes in Syro-Palestine*, Dead Sea Discoveries, Vol.10, No.2, 2003, pp 205-220.
[59] A substantial number of entries in the English translation of the great New Pauly Encyclopaedia, published by E.J.Brill, were translated by myself, as part of the large initial academic translation team; (but not the article "Artemisia").

acolytes underwent there may have been undertaken at various times, and went without any connection to social festivities.

However, in the 19th century, Greek women wanted to create a festival for themselves, and they decided to use the name 'Artemisia' for this. They were no doubt unaware that it was not so used by their ancestors, two thousand years ago. So, by the early 20th century, people began to use the word 'Artemisia' to designate the festival of Artemis.

εἶναι μῆνα καλούμενον παρ' ἡ[μ]ῖν μὲν Ἀρτ[εμισι-
ῶνα παρὰ δὲ Μακεδόσιν καὶ τοῖς λοιποῖς ἔ[θνεσιν
τοῖς Ἑλληνικοῖς καὶ ταῖς ἐν αὐτοῖς πόλεσι[ν
20   Ἀρτεμίσιον, ἐν ᾧ μηνὶ πανηγύρεις τε καὶ ἱερ[ο-
μηνίαι ἐπιτελοῦνται, διαφερόντως δὲ ἐν [τῇ
ἡμετέρᾳ πόλει τῇ τροφῷ τῆς ἰδίας θεοῦ τῆς Ἐφ[εσί-
α]ς· προσῆκον δὲ εἶναι ἡγούμενος ὁ δῆμος [ὁ
Ἐ]φεσίων ὅλον τὸν μῆνα τὸν ἐπώνυμον τοῦ θ[είου
25   ὀ]νόματος εἶναι ἱερὸν καὶ ἀνακεῖσθαι τῇ θεῷ
ἐ]δοκίμασεν δ[ι]ὰ τοῦδε τοῦ ψηφίσματος [κατα-
στῆσ]αι τὴν περὶ αὐτοῦ θρησκείαν· διὸ [δεδόχθαι
ἱερ]ὸν τὸν μῆνα τὸν Ἀρτεμισιῶνα εἶ[ναι πάσας
τ]ὰς ἡμέρας, ἄγεσθαι δὲ ἐπ' αὐταῖς μῆν[α ὅλον
30   δι'] ἔτους τὰς ἑορτὰς καὶ τὴν τῶν Ἀρτεμ[ισίων πανήγυ-
υριν καὶ τὰς ἱερομηνίας, ἅτε τοῦ μηνὸς ὅ[λου ἀνακειμέ-
νου τῇ θεῷ· οὕτω γὰρ ἐπὶ τὸ ἄμεινον τῆς [θεοῦ τιμωμέ-
ν]ης ἡ πόλις ἡμ[ῶν ἐ]νδοξοτέρα τε καὶ εὐδ[αιμονεστέρα
εἰς τὸ[ν ἅπα]ντα διαμενεῖ χ[ρόνον.

Illustration 2 The alleged 'Artemisia' reference from Thucydides, as quoted in the old Wissowa-Pauly Encyclopaedia. Only the word "Artemidia" is there. (Thucydides 3: 104;5)

μνησάμενοι τέρπουσιν, ὅταν καθέσωσιν ἀγῶνα.

" [5] ὅτι δὲ καὶ μουσικῆς ἀγὼν ἦν καὶ ἀγωνιούμενοι

ἐφοίτων ἐν τοῖσδε αὖ δηλοῖ, ἅ ἐστιν ἐκ τοῦ αὐτοῦ

προοιμίου· τὸν γὰρ Δηλιακὸν χορὸν τῶν γυναικῶν

ὑμνήσας ἐτελεύτα τοῦ ἐπαίνου ἐς τάδε τὰ ἔπη, ἐν οἷς καὶ

ἑαυτοῦ ἐπεμνήσθη· "ἀλλ᾽ ἄγεθ᾽, ἱλήκοι μὲν Ἀπόλλων

Ἀρτέμιδι ξύν,   Artemidi = "as to Artemis"

χαίρετε δ᾽ ὑμεῖς πᾶσαι. ἐμεῖο δὲ καὶ μετόπισθε

μνήσασθ᾽, ὁππότε κέν τις ἐπιχθονίων ἀνθρώπων

Illustration 3 Showing how Rudolf Steiner wrote "würde".

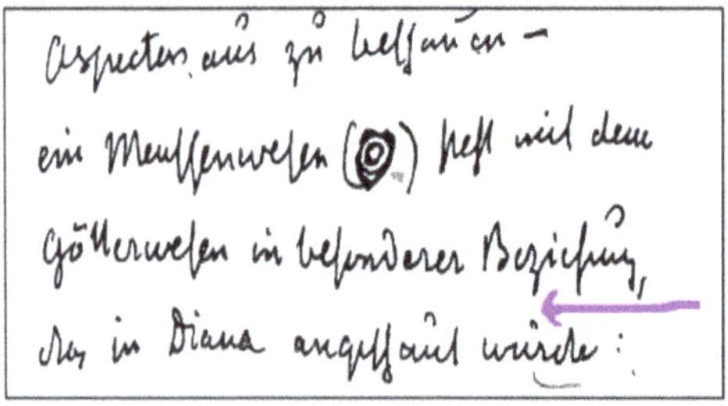

The Ephesos note (extract)

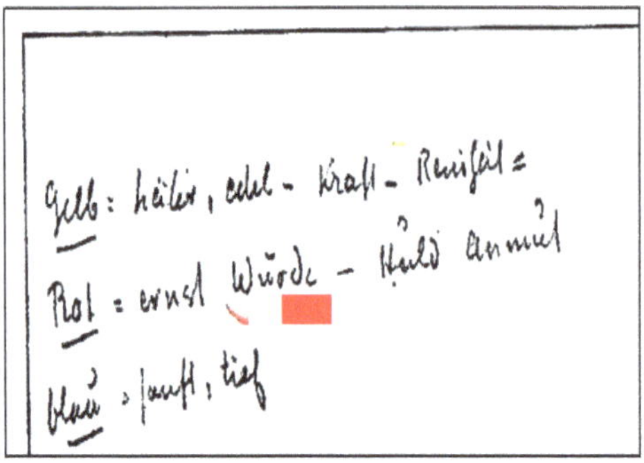

Purple arrow points to the word with rough markings above the 'u'.

The word with the red box underneath is würde: ("ernst würde") not 'wûrde'.

Above: This confirms that the word in the Ephesos note has a scribbled Umlaut = würde.

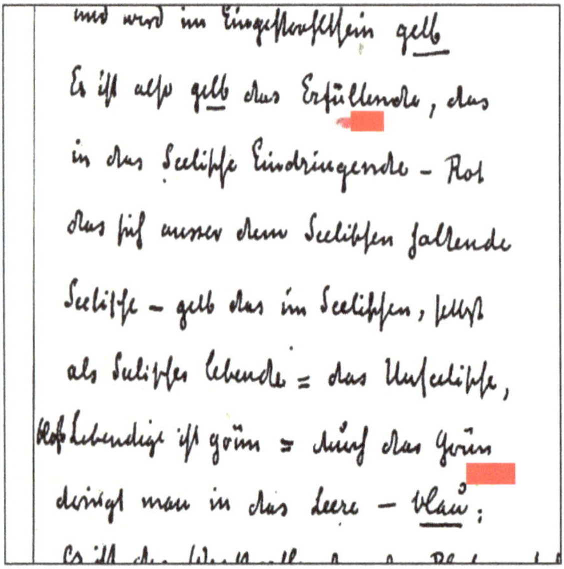

Erfüllende

grün

Again confirming the Ephesos word as 'würde', (not just 'wûrde' with a vowel emphasis over 'u'). Both words with red boxes below, have a scribbled Umlaut = **ü** not û.

Illustration 4 The private notebook entry about 'Isrenum'.
Left: 1st section; on the right is the continuation.

Index

GLOSSARY of some central anthroposophical terms

Aeon: a long evolutionary time. There are seven of these, and we are now in the fourth such. They are called the Saturn, Sun, Moon, Earth (which has two halves, Mars and Mercury) Jupiter, Venus and Vulcan aeons.

Ahriman: an evil entity responsible for the attitude which sees matter as the only thing in creation, denying spiritual reality. It correlates to the Biblical term, Satan.

Angels: spiritual beings who are one aeon ahead of human beings in their evolution.

anthroposophy: a Greek word that literally means 'human-soul wisdom'. In Rudolf Steiner's usage it means the wisdom that can dawn in a person's consciousness, in their spiritual-soul; and which fully manifests when the Spiritual-self is developed.

Archangels: spiritual beings who are two aeons ahead of human beings in their evolution.

astral body: the soul, seen as an aura around the body.

astral realm: the Soul-world, above the ethers, but below the Devachanic realms.

astrality: soul energies, but often it refers mainly to the feelings.

Buddhi Plane: a divine realm more transcendent than Devachan; it is where the Bodhisattvas exist

Consciousness-soul: (see spiritual-soul)

Cosmic Christ: the highest of the 'Powers' or sun-gods.

Devachan: the true heavens above the Soul-world; a Theosophical term from the Sanskrit meaning 'realm of the shining gods'; it is the realm of the archetypal Idea of Plato.

Devachanic aura: the eternal, divine Self, like the soul or astral body, appears as an aura to the seer.

the Double: a term usually referring to the Lower Self.

ego or self or I: the sense of self, but the eternal self is linked to this. Hence the ego is a dual or twofold thing.

egoism or egoistic: not quite the same as the well-known term egotism (which means conceit). Egoism is used by Rudolf Steiner to mean either the state of having a normal earth-centred ego, or for this earthly sense of self behaving in a selfish way.

etheric body: is made of the four ethers and duplicates the physical body's appearance, from which organic matter, such as new cells, are condensed.

ethers: subtle energies which sustain all living things on the Earth. Electricity and magnetism are formed as the ethers decompose.

Group-soul: a spirit-being to whom all the animals of a particular species belong.

intellectual-soul: the rational, logical capacity.

Imagination, Inspiration, Intuition: Latin words for the three types of clairvoyance, but which mean something different in everyday usage in English to the meanings that Rudolf Steiner gives them.

Imagination: the first stage of clairvoyance; can be called 'psychic-image consciousness'. It brings perception of astral or etheric images, (usually means 'fantasy'.)

Imaginations: astral thought-forms.

Inspiration: this can be called 'cosmic-spiritual consciousness', it is a perceiving or 'breathing-in' wisdom, from lower Devachan (In normal English usually this word means a strongly felt creative urge or idea.)

Intuition: this can be called a 'High initiation consciousness'. It is a perceiving of another being by inwardly becoming one with that being. This state allows the seer to perceive at an upper Devachan level. (In normal English this word usually means a semi-psychic awareness of something.)

intuition: can be used by Rudolf Steiner for the above high seership, but it can sometimes appear in English anthroposophical texts in its usual English meaning of 'insights' (translating such German words as 'ahnen').

life-force: an alternative term for ether.

life-force organism: the ether body.

Life-spirit: the divinized etheric body, is made of Devachanic energies.

lower-self: the soul qualities that are tainted with Luciferic or Ahrimanic influences. It can be thought of as threefold, the lower thinking, feeling and will. But Rudolf Steiner also described it as sevenfold, being the lower qualities of the seven classical planets in astrology.

Lucifer: a 'fallen' entity who opposes the intentions of the higher gods, creating an ungrounded, naïve attitude in human beings, but also instils a sense of self and enthusiasm for beauty, art and sensuality.

sentient-soul: the feelings, the emotion capacities of the soul.

soul: appears as an aura, and contains the sentient-soul, intellectual-soul and spiritual-soul.

Spirit-human: the divine forces underlying the physical body, in our subconscious will.

Spiritual-self: the result of the purified and enlightened threefold soul-body or astral body.

spiritual-soul: also translated as 'consciousness soul', and could be called the intuitive soul. This is the soul capacity which underlies intuitive decision-making or intuitive flashes of insight. But it is also the most individualized or 'ego-ic' soul capacity, and can tend towards a hardened self-centredness.

Spiritual-sun: the sun on its soul (or astral) level, behind the physical globe, and also on its actual spiritual level (also referred to as the Devachanic level): these levels comprise many energies and divine beings.

thinking: can be used to mean the exercise of our intelligence, but it is also used to mean any of the three clairvoyant states we can attain.

Illustration credits

1 Colour photo of statue of Artemis:
Wikipedia Commons.
Description: The Temple of Artemis (Diana) by
Ferdinand Knab
Date: 1886
Source: Series "Seven Wonders of the Ancient World"
by Ferdinand Knab
Author: Ferdinand Knab

Cover: Temple of Ephesos
Developed by the author from a line drawing, in *Entwurf einer historishen Architektur*, J.B. Fischer, 1721.

Books by this Author

Living a Spiritual Year: seasonal festivals in both hemispheres (new, expanded edition, 2016)	1992
The Way to the Sacred	2003
The Foundation Stone Meditation: a new commentary	2005
Dramatic Anthroposophy: Identification and contextualization of primary features of Rudolf Steiner's anthroposophy. (PhD thesis)	2005
Two Gems from Rudolf Steiner	2014
The Hellenistic Mysteries & Christianity	2014
Rudolf Steiner Handbook	2014
Horoscope Handbook – a Rudolf Steiner Approach	2015
The Meaning of the Goetheanum Windows	2016
The Lost Zodiac of Rudolf Steiner	2016
Rudolf Steiner's Esoteric Christianity in the Grail painting by Anna May	2017
The Vidar Flame Column – its meaning from Rudolf Steiner	2017
Rudolf Steiner on Leonardo's *Last Supper*	2017
Blessed - Rudolf Steiner on the Beatitudes	2018
Rudolf Steiner's First Class Verses	2019
The Soul's Calendar - annotated with Commentary	2020
The Soul's Calendar - pocket edition	2020
The Apocalyptic Seals from Rudolf Steiner	2020

Also, under the pen-name Damien Pryor:

Website: www.rudolfsteinerstudies.com

This site has information on all of these books, as well as free downloads of various essays, and a link to the author's ARTPRINTS page, which offers esoteric diagrams and great classical works of art which are relevant to the understanding of anthroposophy.

www.ingramcontent.com/pod-product-compliance
Lightning Source LLC
Chambersburg PA
CBHW050819090426
42737CB00021B/3447